Great
Expectations

Elaine
Tyler
May

Great Expectations

*Marriage
and Divorce
in Post-Victorian
America*

The University of Chicago Press
Chicago and London

ELAINE TYLER MAY is a
social historian who has taught at
Princeton University and is currently
teaching American Studies at the
University of Minnesota.

The University of Chicago Press, Chicago 60637
The University of Chicago Press, Ltd., London

84 83 82 81 80   5 4 3 2 1

To Lary
for not having too many
Great Expectations

Library of Congress Cataloging in Publication Data
May, Elaine Tyler.
    Great expectations.
    Includes bibliographical references and index.
    1. Marriage—United States—History.   2.
Divorce—United States—History—19th century.
3. Divorce—United States—History—20th century.
4. United States—Social conditions—1865–1918.
5. United States Social conditions—1918–1932.
I. Title.
HQ536.M37   306.8'0973   8–10590
ISBN 0–226–51166–9

Contents

Acknowledgments

I am grateful to a number of people who gave generously of their time and talents to help me strengthen this work—the weaknesses are entirely my own. My warmest gratitude goes to Stephan Thernstrom, whose critical eye and constant encouragement have followed this project since its inception, and pushed me toward his own high standards of scholarly excellence. Several others read and criticized all or parts of the manuscript at various stages, including Gary Nash, Dorothy Ross, Lois Banner, John Modell, Judith Smith, Estelle Freedman, and Lewis Erenberg.

Financial support for this project in its first phase as a doctoral dissertation came from a Ford Foundation Dissertation Fellowship in Women's Studies, the California State Graduate Fellowship Commission, and the Mabel Wilson Richards Foundation of UCLA. A generous summer research grant from Princeton University made it possible for me to expand the scope of the study. I would also like to thank my research assistant at Princeton, Wendy Healy, for her many hours of work and for gathering the New Jersey data. The staff of the Los Angeles County Archives gave me a desk of my own and never complained about digging out dusty boxes of old divorce files.

Friends and family provided much needed assistance. Special thanks to Susan Camber for her unwavering moral support, and to Omri Shochatovitz whose friendship and immeasurable help made it possible for me to finish this project. My mother Lillian Tyler spent hours of her own professional life with her grandchildren to give me more time to work. My father Edward Tyler took time from his busy medical practice to read and criticize the study—my greatest sadness is that he did not live to see it appear in print. Michael May provided nine years of healthy interruptions, Daniel May contributed two years of worthy scribbling upon my rough drafts, and Sarah May was born just in time to prevent me from becoming totally obsessed with the final stages of this project. My greatest thanks goes to Lary May. As husband and colleague, he has made contributions to this work on all levels. Without his sharing of both scholarly and family concerns, this book would never have been written.

Introduction

In the Superior Court of Los Angeles in 1920, Lorimer Linganfield, a respectabe barber, filed for a divorce. Although his
wife, Marsha, held him in "high regard and esteem as her
husband," there were "evidences of indiscretion" in her conduct. She wore a new bathing suit, "designed especially for the
purpose of exhibiting to the public the shape and form of her
body." To his further humiliation, she was "beset with a desire to sing and dance at cafes and restaurants for the entertainment of the public." When Lorimer complained about her
"appetite for beer and whisky" and extravagant tastes for luxury, she replied that he was "not the only pebble on the beach,
she had a millionare 'guy' who would by her all the clothes,
automobiles, diamonds and booze that she wanted." But the
ultimate insult was her refusal to have any sexual intercourse,
claiming that she did not want any "dirty little brats around
her." The judge was sympathetic, and Lorimer Linganfield
won his suit.[1]

At first glance, this case appears to be an extreme example
of an unfortunate union between a morally righteous man and a
woman whose behavior was something less than proper. But
on closer examination, it becomes clear that the Linganfields
were plagued by a number of problems that were especially
acute in the decades surrounding the turn of the century in
America. Marsha Linganfield was shedding the mores of the
Victorian past and eager to enter new areas of work and play
that had been closed to women previously. Her husband may
well have been attracted to the vivacious flapper he wooed and
wed. But like many men of his generation, he expected her to
settle into proper wifely decorum after their marriage. When
she failed to maintain a modest and frugal demeanor, he began

to lose face with his patrons and customers. Marsha's flamboyant behavior tarnished his impeccable reputation. Yet the
young wife felt constrained by a prudish husband, and flaunted
her adventurous spirit in spite of his ardent pleas. The tension
was more than the couple could bear, and their marriage fell
apart.

During the late nineteenth and early twentieth centuries,
American marriages began to collapse at an unprecedented
rate. Between 1867 and 1929, the population of the United
States grew 300 percent, the number of marriages increased
400 percent, and the divorce rate rose 2,000 percent. By the
end of the 1920s, more than one in every six marriages termi-
nated in court.[2] Public debate over the causes of divorce began
over a century ago, among clergy and moralists who blamed
individual depravity. But well before 1900, observers began to
cite social forces as contributing to the problem. Moral tur-
pitude was simply not enough to explain the sudden leap in
marital dissolutions, which brought this country the dubious
distinction of having the highest rate of marital breakdown in
the world. The personal crises of people like the Linganfields
reflected a much larger crisis in the society: the birth pangs of
modern American culture as we know it today. But as yet we
have very little understanding of this profound development.
What caused the American divorce rate to skyrocket so dramatically during these years?

The first systematic efforts to explain the phenomenon came
in the late nineteenth century, from the new profession of social science. In 1897, a Columbia University professor, Walter
Willcox, claimed that a major reason for the rising divorce rate
was the "emancipation of women." As more women entered
the economy, he argued, they became less dependent on their
husbands, causing the "economic bond" to be "relaxed."
Marriage, he wrote,

is fundamentally grounded on the differences, physical, intellectual, and moral, between the sexes. Consequently a
marriage almost invariably recognizes and emphasizes these
differences, through varieties of work and function. So far as
the training of the two sexes prior to the marriage has been
identical, one or the other must be ill fitted for that life; so far
as women's work has become masculine, her ability to make
and keep a home happy is diminished.[3]

Despite the professor's judgmental tone, his perceptions were astute. The sharp separation of the sexes that Willcox believed to be essential for domestic tranquility was, indeed, breaking down. But this need not portend doom, as Willcox implied. In fact, within a decade, sociologists came to view the trend more favorably.

James P. Lichtenberger of the University of Pennsylvania, for example, writing in 1909, also linked women's emancipation to the rising divorce rate. But unlike Willcox he applauded the change:

Marriage is no longer the only vocation open to her and for which she is qualified. She is not forced into marriage as her only means of support. . . . If marriage is a failure, she does not face the alternative of endurance or starvation. The way is open for independent support. . . . She is no longer compelled to accept support or yield to the tyranny of a husband whose conduct is a menace to her health and happiness.[4]

Lichtenberger expressed the sentiments of many reformers and feminists who hailed divorce as a new advance in freeing victimized women from the shackles of marital bondage. Critics, however, deplored the development, bemoaning the collapse of America's most sacred institution, the home. But alarmists and advocates alike generally recognized that divorce, for better or for worse, was part of modern urban life.[5]

Although the emphasis on personal depravity eventually retired from the forefront of the divorce controversy, scholars as well as moralists continued to infuse their writings with value judgments. By the 1930s, sociologists pinned the phenomenon to "vast social forces" which ultimately caused marriages to collapse. The city itself was the main villain. Whether it was the "mobility, dense population, and . . . anonymity" of the urban environment or the "breakdown of neighborhood control," these observers believed that the "repressive and coercive control of the primary group" was lost, freeing the individual from "the usual social restraints." The result, they argued, was that city life fostered juvenile delinquency, mental illness, and a high rate of divorce. It is true that all of these phenomena are more highly concentrated in metropolitan areas; but no direct causal link between certain features of urban living and the emergence of these problems has ever been conclusively proven.[6]

Mistaken assumptions concerning the causes of divorce also inhibited the effectiveness of efforts to deal with the problem.

Most of those concerned about the issue, blind to the extent of its cultural dimensions, believed the divorce rate could be manipulated. Some hoped that moral suasion would suffice to save the family, and called for resistance against the corruptions of modern life. But it became readily apparent that moral suasion would not work. Divorce reformers then turned to the coercive powers of existing institutions, especially the legal system. Both proponents and opponents of divorce believed that the rate of marital dissolution could be controlled through effective use of the law.

Conservatives hoped to make it extremely difficult for couples to terminate their marriages. Liberals and women's rights advocates wished to utilize the legal system to enable unhappily married people—particularly wives—to escape the bonds of wedlock. Both strategies were a sharp break from the rather haphazard practices of the past. Throughout much of the nineteenth century, most states provided for decrees of divorce to be granted through legislatures. As the population increased and these assemblies became involved in many complex functions, they began to delegate responsibility for granting dissolutions of marriage to the courts. The grounds were often unspecified; several states enacted "omnibus" clauses which gave courts or governing bodies the power to grant a divorce for any reason, if they felt there was adequate justification. A general trend toward liberalization paralleled a slow but steady increase in the divorce rate up to the Civil War. But after the war, as broken marriages became more frequent, these measures were no longer adequate. Many people began to notice the phenomenon and become alarmed.[7]

Between 1889 and 1906, as the divorce rate began to accelerate rapidly, state legislatures across the country, most of them in the East, enacted more than one hundred pieces of restrictive marriage and divorce legislation in an effort to stem the tide. Five states established laws for the defense of an absent party in a divorce suit; fifteen states forbade remarriage until one or two years after a final decree; eighteen states increased the residence requirement prior to filing suit; and six states eliminated certain grounds for marital dissolution. Washington, D.C., and New York permitted divorce only in the case of adultery. In 1895, South Carolina went further than any other state, and banned divorce altogether. The eastern seaboard was the center of legal reaction, where most of the restrictive legislation was passed. Easterners also waged a vigorous crusade for uniform divorce laws, campaigning ardently for strict statutes across the country. During this national mobilization, western states were constantly berated for their legislative laxity, which allegedly fostered family disintegration.[8]

New Jersey was among the most conservative states in terms of divorce. It was home of some of the most active proponents.of a uniform national law; its governor made strict divorce statutes one of his primary concerns. As late as 1923, the only two legal grounds for marital dissolution in New Jersey were adultery and desertion. When cruelty was added, it created an enormous furor in the state, even though it had long since ceased to be a major national issue. Oddly enough, however, the new law made little difference in the state. Most suits were still filed on the original two grounds, even after cruelty was added.[9]

The inability of New Jersey legislation to stem the tide of divorce reflected a national pattern: all across the country it became more difficult to obtain a divorce. If these laws had been effective in curbing the trend, we should expect to find at least a slowing down of the divorce rate. But this did not occur. A study of the effect of legal changes written in 1932 stated, "A detailed analysis . . . of divorce legislation from the Civil War to the present time shows that the number of changes has been many but their importance slight . . . there has been a minor tendency towards increasing strictness. Since the divorce rate has multiplied fivefold notwithstanding, the legal influences were evidently negligible."[10]

Nearly every study of divorce and the law has concluded that legal changes have little or no impact upon the rate of marital dissolutions.[11] Whatever the laws might be, people who wish to terminate their unions will do so, and fit into the legal structure that is available. Perhaps the greatest testimony to this fact comes from South Carolina, where divorce was abolished. Obviously, the law had an effect on the divorce rate—it brought it down to zero. But it clearly did not keep families together. In fact, South Carolina eventually had to devise laws pertaining to how much a married man could bequeath to his mistress![12]

In contrast to New Jersey and South Carolina, California

was in the vanguard of liberalism in matters of divorce when in 1872 the legislature codified broad provisions for marital dissolution, alimony, custody, and community property. These statutes remained unchanged for several decades. As in other western states, Progressives held political control in California at the time.[13] They did not wish to use the coercive powers of the state to keep unhappy couples together. Rather, they believed that the best way to prevent divorce was to remove the corrupting elements in society that threatened family values. But these efforts at moral crusading were no more effective in stemming the tide than the legislative measures enacted in eastern states. In fact, the West has always had a slightly higher divorce rate than the East. Yet in spite of regional variations, the rising divorce rate during the early twentieth century was truly a national phenomenon. Clearly, marital failure was not determined or heavily influenced by legal manipulation. Both stringency and leniency, however, can be seen as different means toward achieving the same end. Liberals and conservatives alike hoped to see the family strengthened rather than weakened in the transition to modern life. But all their efforts were futile, for they failed to understand the underlying causes of marital breakdown.

Scholars have perpetuated a distorted view of divorce by examining the phenomenon in a narrow context. By far their most common assumption is the notion that the rising rate of martial dissolution is tied to the movement for women's rights. Although the trends do coincide, their connection is not at all clear. Those who try to explain the rapid upsurge in divorce by pointing to newly liberated wives opting out of wedlock drastically oversimplify the matter. Even the best and most recent works on the subject generally rest upon the common wisdom of liberal politics and a confident faith in progress: divorce may not be a pleasant business, but it is a healthy safety valve in modern life, especially for women.[14] William O'Neill, for example, in his pioneering study of the divorce controversy, described the situation as it had evolved prior to 1900. Women married at a later age than their mothers had; they were better educated, had fewer children, and were more likely to support themselves. "These were the 'new women' who were so often talked about, and their special characteristics might well have made them more susceptible to divorce."

Their "strength and self-assurance" made them "less tolerant of a poor marriage, and more confident of [their] ability to survive outside it."[15] O'Neill suggests that as more women entered the economy, fewer would feel compelled to tolerate unsatisfying unions merely for the sake of security. This may well have been true. But if his argument is taken one step further, it is logical to presume that given wider choices, more and more women would decide against marriage altogether. One cannot jump to this conclusion, however, before carefully analyzing the relationship between changing roles for women and divorce. For if female emancipation was the main reason for the increasing frequency of divorce, one would expect to find that, as women's rights advanced during the twentieth century, the marriage rate would decrease and the marriage age would continue to rise.

In fact, the opposite occurred. Contradicting the assumption that more divorce meant less interest in marriage, between 1900 and 1920 the proportion of the eligible population choosing to marry rose along with the divorce rate (see table 1). Moreover, the marriage age declined for both sexes (see table 2). Oddly enough, with more alternatives opening up for new types of experiences, more people were choosing to marry. What gave rise to this increasing inclination toward matrimony? It is quite likely that the same forces sparking the marriage rate also led to the rising divorce rate. Both trends are, in a sense, two sides of the same coin.

It is impossible to comprehend the marriage and divorce phenomenon without a broad cultural analysis. The home does not exist in isolation; one cannot begin to fathom the dynamics of private life without a careful look at public institutions as well. Similarly, an examination of women's roles alone leaves out half of the story; one of the most neglected areas of social history is the changing role of men. A full-blown inquiry into the problem calls for close attention to men as well as women, to marriage as well as divorce, and to public as well as private concerns. Woven together, these various elements provide the tapestry of modern life that emerged out of the threads of historical change. This backdrop is essential for unraveling the complicated strands of individual experience: what post-Victorian Americans seemed to want out of marriage, and why they were increasingly unable to achieve it.

The major sources for this study are divorce proceedings themselves. I have gathered three samples of court records, two from Los Angeles and one comparative sample from New Jersey. The Los Angeles documents include five hundred cases filed in the 1880s, and another five hundred from 1920.[16] The New Jersey sample includes two hundred twenty-five divorces filed throughout the state in 1920. These two locales provide legal as well as regional variation, since California was one of the most lenient divorce states and New Jersey among the most stringent. The divorce laws in Los Angeles remained virtually unchanged over the forty-year period. There were six legal grounds for dissolving a marriage: desertion, extreme cruelty, willful neglect to provide, adultery, intemperance, and conviction of a felony. Annulments could be granted for fraud, coercion, or a previous marriage still in effect. New Jersey in 1920 recognized only two legal grounds for divorce: adultery and desertion. These East Coast records have the advantage of including both urban and rural residents, as well as documenting cases filed under a radically different legal code. By probing underneath the legal grounds, we can compare the issues causing marital friction in California and New Jersey.

Los Angeles provides an ideal locale for studying the problem. Although there is no such thing as a "typical" American city, Los Angeles had a number of characteristics that make it a particularly useful place for examining marriage and divorce during the turn-of-the-century decades. For one thing, the rapid rise of the divorce rate coincided with the growth of the city into a major urban center. Between 1870 and 1920, the population grew from 5,728 to 576,673—a hundredfold increase in fifty years. In the 1880s, the decade from which the first divorce sample was drawn, Los Angeles was still sparsely populated. But it was already experiencing a land boom and a massive influx of migrants, largely native-born Americans from the Middle West.[17] By the 1920s, it was a booming metropolis displaying a number of distinctly twentieth-century characteristics.

Because Los Angeles urbanized later than the industrial centers of the East, it was, in a sense, born modern. Features often associated with Los Angeles, including its suburban sprawl and its fame as a center for radiating mass culture, are not really unique to Southern California. Rather, Los Angeles has been something of a pacesetter for modern urban life. It has had no monopoly on suburbia, movies, or the Hollywood style—it simply developed some of these dimensions before other cities. Due to the timing of its growth, Los Angeles has always been a prototypical twentieth-century American city. For this reason, it is an appropriate locale for examining modern urban culture in a purified form. This does not, however, make it a peculiar city. Indeed, it is well to heed James Q. Wilson's warning against dwelling too heavily on the uniqueness of Los Angeles, for "we are, in essence . . . one nation."[18]

Not surprisingly, Los Angeles has had its share of divorce. But in this, too, the city is not really so far removed from the national norm. Divorce has always been concentrated much more heavily in cities than in rural areas, and the rates of marital dissolution have been highest in the West. The divorce rate in Los Angeles has been consistently high, but not extraordinarily so. In 1916, for example, Los Angeles had one divorce for every five marriages. This was higher than the national average, but not higher than the rate for other western cities. San Francisco had a rate of one in four, while Chicago, with comparable divorce laws, had only one in seven.[19] A high rate of divorce, then, is not unique to the city, but another feature of twentieth-century life that it contains.

In the early decades of this modern metropolis, who was getting divorced? Contrary to the commonly held view that divorce was concentrated among certain social classes, the data gathered for this study indicate that marital breakdown could happen to anyone. Both Los Angeles samples include men and women from all segments of the population. Nearly every racial, ethnic, and occupational group is represented, in proportions approximating the composition of the city as a whole (see tables 3 and 4). The preponderance of Midwesterners in Los Angeles is reflected in the samples, Protestant Americans who comprised the bulk of the city's population had their share of divorce (see table 5). In terms of nativity, we find that the proportion of foreign born in the samples is slightly below their percentage in the city's population. Natives appear somewhat more prone to marital dissolution than immigrants.

If the samples are divided along racial lines, the results are much the same. The racial composition of the 1920 Los

Angeles divorce sample approximates that of the married control group as well as the population as a whole (see tables 3 and 4). Blacks appear to be slightly underrepresented, and individuals with Spanish surnames slightly overrepresented; but the numbers in these categories are too small to be statistically significant. In the 1880s, however, when Mexicans still comprised a fairly large proportion of the population, white natives appear more often in the divorce sample, and Spanish-surnamed individuals more often in the control group. Perhaps this is due to the prohibitions against divorce in the Roman Catholic Church. Or perhaps in the 1880s, the Mexican community in Los Angeles was still culturally intact. For whatever reason, we find less divorce among this group in the 1880s than their apparent percentage of the married population; but by 1920, when Protestant Americans had taken over the city, this no longer held true.

The individuals included in these samples comprise a very diverse group. They had only one thing in common: all experienced marital difficulties that brought them into court. The records they left provide the basis for this study. Each case has been analyzed and coded into over fifty categories relating to the participants, the nature of the litigation, and the marital difficulties. Complaints mentioned to support the legal grounds in both locales are divided into over one hundred of the most common problems reported in the proceedings. When these files are opened and the struggles of the participants laid bare, the numbers and statistics suddenly come to life. These documents are often extremely detailed and explicit, for unlike today, mutual incompatibility was not a valid ground for divorce. If an aggrieved spouse failed to convince the court that the complaints were extensive and serious, the petition for divorce was denied. This obligation to persuade, though it may have forced distorted accusations in order to prove that there was a "guilty" party, created a positive advantage for the investigator: the legal structure compelled the spouses to express their grievances against each other in court. In many cases, litigants unleashed their deepest feelings and resentments—a rare thing to find in public records.

The wide variety of complaints, as well as the litigants' deeply personal and detailed testimonies, reflect a remarkable degree of candor. Spouses were not forced to lie or mold their difficulties into a particular formula in order to fit the laws. Rather, the categories were broad enough to include virtually every type of conflict that erupted in these unfortunate unions. Even in New Jersey where the laws were quite strict, the records contain as much variety as the California proceedings. In fact, those from New Jersey are often even more revealing, since each litigant in a divorce suit was interviewed by a state official, and the transcripts were entered in the files. Included within the records from both locales are extensive complaint forms, numerous letters between the spouses and their friends entered as evidence, and statements of witnesses, doctors, or social workers. The wealth of evidence entered in the cases makes it possible to piece together elements of the individuals' lives and discover their unfulfilled expectations.

These types of materials add qualitative dimensions to quantitative data. Although all the information included in the records has been analyzed by computer, the resulting statistics and tables are not the answers. They merely raise provocative questions. Quantitative methodology is useful in finding out how people lived; but it rarely reveals what they thought. For ideas and attitudes, it is often necessary to rely on members of the elite, social leaders, and published writers. Divorce records provide a rare opportunity to discover the beliefs and feelings of ordinary Americans. Each unique testimony itself serves as a microscope through which it is possible to examine the effects of historical change on individual lives. These men and women expressed their deepest hopes and disappointments at a time of profound personal crisis, unaware that their struggles would serve any purpose beyond their own predicaments. Yet they provided a means for future generations to gain a deeper understanding of the changing experiences of men and women in modern America—why they were more eager to marry, and more willing to divorce.

I

Tradition in Transition in the Late Nineteenth Century

One

Los Angeles and the Victorian Synthesis

Today, Los Angeles is noted for its modernism—a city that has always been in the vanguard of cultural change, pioneering new forms of popular culture, consumer styles, and sex roles. It is associated with innovative and experimental patterns of marriage and family life and is well known for its high rate of divorce. Ironically, however, this prototypical twentieth-century metropolis was settled by Victorians who endeavored to create a city that would keep their traditions intact. These native Americans were deeply concerned about the social and moral tone of their newfound community. They hoped to protect it from the unwelcome influences that appeared to be eroding the industrial centers of the East. Los Angeles had one great advantage over these older urban areas: newness. Between 1880 and 1920, this burgeoning city on the western edge of the frontier was filled with migrants, mostly from the Middle West, many of whom were reared in the world the Victorians made. They brought their hopes for a better life to this "city of heart's desire," and shaped the development of the region in tune with their past values and future wishes.[1] In order to understand how they molded their environment, we must look to the tradition they carried with them across the continent. What was this Victorian culture?

Twentieth-century Americans have been guilty of heaping scorn upon the heads of their Victorian forebears. In an attempt to define the present as more liberated than the past, Victorians have received more than their share of pity and disdain. Some criticisms of nineteenth-century culture are well deserved, to be sure. But others are downright mythical inventions of a modern society looking for a usable present in an unusable past. All too often, the profound historical transformation known as the Victorian breakdown is reduced to a

15

superficial emphasis on the "revolution in manners and morals" beginning in turn-of-the-century America. This facile ex-
planation rests on the assumption that Victorianism was first
and foremost a moral code, which found its expression within
the walls of the home. Although this may be essentially true,
Victorianism was much more. Notions of prudery and pure
womanhood have blinded us to the totality of nineteenth-
century life, with its intricate ideological and institutional
framework. It is crucial to look beyond the level of domestic
morality and probe the entire world view that set the cultural
tone for the nation. Only then can we begin to comprehend the
changes that ushered in the twentieth century, in Los Angeles
as well as the rest of the country, and brought an end to the
world of the Victorians.[2]

First of all, who were the Victorians? It is not clear how
many nineteenth-century Americans actually fit the model, but
we must attempt to place them in some temporal and geographical context. Several studies locate the seeds of Victorian
culture on the East Coast, in the affluent segments of the urban
population in the latter decades of the eighteenth century.
Economic diversity had begun to give rise to a complex and
stratified social order. Men no longer automatically inherited
their fathers' land and worked alongside women to maintain
family farms. Rather, individuals coming of age often left the
parental domain, moving into new communities and entering
new occupations. The growing cities attracted large groups of
unattached working men, as well as entrepreneurs with
families who endeavored to secure lucrative economic positions. At the upper strata emerged a group of well-to-do merchants and professionals. It was this class that began to define
the cultural form of Victorianism. Men usually worked in a
separate sphere, away from their homes. Their wives comprised America's first leisure class, with the time and money to
develop a genteel way of life. These were the men and women
whose descendants would fill the ranks of the Protestant
churches, engage in the various campaigns to reform society,
and stand at the forefront of economic development and west-
ward movement. Individuals born into this tradition became
leaders of the institutions that set the norms for the nation.
They spread across the continent, bringing their way of life to
the constantly expanding frontier.[3]

As early as the 1820s and 1830s, Victorian values were widely articulated in a profusion of advice books, popular stories, journals, dime novels, sermons and exhortations of various sorts. Social norms expressed in these forms do not always describe the reality of day-to-day living, but they do suggest a common ideal toward which the society, as a whole, might aspire. The Victorian formula, set by native-born white Protestant Americans of the middle classes, reflected the spirit of independence and self-denial that was believed to be the key to progress. Their world view contained very specific prescriptions for individual behavior, expecially pertaining to the proper duties and functions of the sexes. The removal of production from the household gave rise to definite notions of distinct male and female spheres. But it did not necessarily signal a total and unbridgeable gap between domestic and economic endeavors. It is precisely here that we can begin to discern the integration of public and private roles that informed the Victorian ethos.

Throughout most of the nineteenth century, men and women were taught to fulfill separate, but vitally interdependent functions. Millions of young men knew the formula, expounded most widely by Horatio Alger, that luck, pluck, ambition, and self-control were the ingredients necessary to become self-made. They learned in church, at home, and in the popular literature what was expected of American manhood. The key element was moral autonomy: total control over one's instincts as well as independent pursuit of one's calling. Perhaps the core of this code was economic self-mastery. Ideally, a man would be his own boss, own his own property, and control his own means of production. The industrious man worked without need of external restraints. Using his freedom to compete in an open economy, he served his own best interests as well as those of his family, community, and nation. The essence of this entrepreneurial ethos was in tune with the republican spirit of individual liberty. A striving man was the perfect citizen, for his ambition furthered, rather than hindered, the goal of national progress.

In contrast, women learned that "the domestic fireside is the great guardian of society against the excess of human passions." It was the wife's duty to maintain a home environment free from sensuality, to help protect husbands and sons from

dissipation. If men were not properly disciplined, they might
lead the country to economic stagnation. In this wider sense,
the woman's role involved more than mere housekeeping; it
was vital to the future of the nation. Accordingly, boys learned
from an early age that "nothing is better calculated to preserve
a young man from contamination of low pleasures and pursuits
than frequent intercourse [i.e., social interaction] with the
more refined and virtuous of the other sex," which would raise
them "above those sordid and sensual considerations which
hold such sway over men." The man's duty was to extend the
asceticism he learned from women at home into the economy.
There he would contribute to building a strong industrial state,
and in turn become personally successful.[4]

Perceptive scholars have found in Victorianism a philo-
sophical unity between personal behavior and nation building.
The spirit of republicanism that fired the fuels of American
expansion in the early decades of the nineteenth century linked
individual endeavor to the march of progress. But this sense of
purpose did not end with ascetic discipline and the well-
documented separation of the sexes. We lose sight of the integrated nature of the nineteenth-century community if we focus
too narrowly on differentiated sex roles and the split between
home and work. Rampant individualism never entirely re-
placed communal concerns; men and women both had vital
functions outside as well as inside the home. In the first place,
the ideology of domesticity and progress implied an organic
connection. The home, or "female sphere," interacted in a
fundamental way with the world beyond. Middle-class women
of the northern towns and cities were the ones who filled the
churches, led the reform movements, worked among the poor
in their communities, and provided numerous charity and
welfare services. Although they were not engaged in economic
pursuits, these women were not confined within the walls of
the house.[5]

Men, too, participated in numerous activities which modify
the notion of obsessive competition. Alexis de Tocqueville,
while noting the atomized nature of the American economy in
the 1830s, also documented the proliferation of all sorts of
voluntary associations. These ranged from trade organizations
and guilds to various church and civic concerns. Even secret
societies such as the Masons served to strengthen community

ties and provide functions of mutual benefit. These attest to a spirit of cooperation manifest among like-minded individuals. In the same sense that self-reliance was to negate the need for external controls, voluntarism was to render widespread governmental machinery unnecessary. Individualism geared toward community responsibility was to keep the society running smoothly.[6]

A prime example of nineteenth-century Americans' public orientation was the time and energy devoted to political and religious activities. Beginning in the Jacksonian period, these were increasingly expressed in social and communal forms. With the end of property qualifications for voting, elections became mass events. Public speakers and candidates gathered huge crowds, and a solid 80 to 90 percent of the eligible voters turned out at the polls. This astounding level of participation remained consistent until the 1890s. At the same time, worship became less private. As waves of revivals swept the country throughout the nineteenth century, religious gatherings became mass events. Prayers and conversions turned into public testimonies of faith. The enthusiasm that went into political rallies, elections, religious revivals, and church attendance suggest that the nineteenth century was not as narrow and private an era as is often assumed.[7]

Religion and politics, moreover, were not entirely separate spheres of life—nor were they disconnected from domestic or economic endeavors. Women combined their religious values with political impulses, extending the sphere of "true womanhood" out into the community. Although they could not vote, one need only glance at the numerous and widespread reform movements to find women consistently in the forefront. They also took their moral and religious activities into the streets of the poor, providing charity for the "worthy" and uplift for the others. The role of moral guardian, then, gave women vital public functions. They led political crusades, conducted welfare services where few governmental agencies intervened, filled the ranks of the churches, and held considerable influence both at home and in the community. Men, too, fused their political, religious, and economic activities. Voting often followed the lines of church membership, and the best jobs were usually awarded to those working-class individuals who demonstrated proof of sobriety and piety. Although such favors were not necessarily benevolent, these efforts do reflect a certain unity of purpose. An integrated concept of civic participation, which tied religion, politics, work, and home into an organic ideological whole, is crucial to our understanding of Victorianism. There were indeed tensions in the complex relations between the sexes and the classes, but these formed the dynamics of social interaction.[8]

Victorianism was without question an important force in nineteenth-century America; but not all Americans were Victorians. Obviously, the code briefly sketched above was virtually irrelevant for much of the working class and many of the ethnic groups who also inhabited urban centers. Although some individuals from these groups did conform to the Victorian family pattern, join churches and voluntary associations, and attain a measure of upward mobility, many did not. Most families with limited resources never experienced the economic autonomy that lay at the center of the Victorian success ethic. The men were rarely self-made entrepreneurs; usually they were dependent upon whoever owned the company or the land where they labored. Their wives rarely had the luxury to be full-time moral guardians of the home; they often worked with their children in menial occupations, pooling their earnings. If they did not have outside employment, they worked in their own homes much as servants did in more affluent residences. Rather than joining charity work or temperance crusades, these families were often the recipients—or victims—of such efforts. For most, Victorian gentility was unthinkable; model sex roles were not only beyond their reach, they were probably not even considered desirable.

The American work ethic with its emphasis on self-denial and asceticism was not particularly appealing to immigrant families and others who came from preindustrial backgrounds. They often had traditions of public and private life that were quite distinct from their genteel neighbors. Many preferred dances or camaraderie at the corner saloon to church picnics or temperance meetings. For workers, Sunday was often the only day for frivolous amusement, and their raucous Sabbath behavior was particularly galling to their pious "betters." On the job as well, traditions were often at odds. Immigrants were accustomed to working according to the task, the season, or the sun—not the time clock imposed by industrial discipline and enforced by their Victorian employers. What appeared as slothfulness in work or degeneracy in leisure alarmed the more genteel members of the community. The activities of these unruly elements might not only hinder productivity and slow the wheels of progress; they threatened to bring down the entire social order as well.[9]

Tensions between those inside and those outside the Victorian construct often provided the dynamics for public and political activity. For instance, native elites frequently clashed with immigrant political machines in controversies that reflected fundamentally different cultural values. Battle lines were drawn between Protestants and Catholics, converted and unconverted, native and immigrant, sober and intemperate, moral and immoral, successful and slothful. Yet in spite of these polarities, social and economic hegemony remained in the hands of the urban middle and upper classes, who continued to hold their familial ethics as the ideal for society.

The efforts of these native-born Americans, however, were not aimed at maintaining a rigid class exclusiveness. In fact, Victorians waged a vigorous campaign to bring outsiders into the fold. They used every means of persuasion or coercion within their power to encourage, or even force, conformity to the code. As employers, they directed the extent of upward mobility by rewarding the virtuous and holding back the recalcitrant. Often a worker needed to demonstarte proof of temperance or church membership in order to be hired. Those known for their sobriety and industry might obtain loans from employers or fellow church members, enabling some workers to attain entrepreneurial status. Others who were deemed unworthy owing to their adherence to a preindustrial work pattern might have trouble finding any job at all. Insistence on traditional holidays or inability to conform to time-clock routines might ruin a worker's chances for secure employment. Strong incentives to meet the requirements of industrial discipline were put before employees; often it made the difference between upward mobility and economic insecurity. Ambitious "outsiders" realized that the most effective means of gaining the fruits of the American system was to assimilate into the dominant cultural milieu. In this way, the tensions between those inside and those outside the Victorian construct were often eased by the premeability of the barrier between them.[10]

True to the spirit of democracy, virtuous individuals from any class could join the respectable community, provided they lived according to the dominant ethos. Workers as workers were not held in disdain if they upheld proper sex roles and domestic duties. Rather, the Victorians were most alarmed by evidence of group power, such as labor unions, or public disorder, such as vice districts. These types of organizations and institutions posed a direct threat to the familial values and voluntaristic ethos that guided the Protestant middle classes—and kept them in positions of power. Even more disconcerting, the very fact that outsiders could gain entrance suggested that those within the fold might lose the benefits of insider status if they did not maintain a constant and unwavering adherence to the code. A Victorian who became a degenerate was an outcast from the respectable community. Everyone knew that downward mobility could take other forms besides a loss of economic status.[11]

During the late nineteenth century, symptoms of cultural decay were only faintly visible. The strength of Victorianism continued undiminished, despite increasing conflicts between labor and capital and a massive influx of immigrants. If anything, these challenges to the culture merely spurred the Victorians on to extend and solidify their influence. Whenever native Americans felt that their time-honored values needed to be reinvigorated, they looked to the West. The frontier always seemed to hold the promise of a perfect future where virtuous individuals could civilize the wilderness and create harmonious communities.[12] In the decades following the Civil War, anxious Victorians looked again toward the frontier for regeneration. With the continent all but conquered, their vision turned to the Pacific Coast. There a new city was taking shape, far from the chaos of the urban East. With hopes of blending Victorian familial values with the fruits of modern progress, Americans began heading to Los Angeles.

Two
Early Divorce in the City of the Angels

Los Angeles provided an ideal setting for restless Victorians looking for something new. Until after the Civil War, it was a rural community of fewer than 6,000 inhabitants, mainly Mexican and Gringo farmers and ranchers. Between 1870 and 1880 the population doubled, with an influx of farmers and merchants from the East. During the eighties, the completion of railroad lines spurred a land boom, beginning the flood of businessmen and professionals who would ultimately transform the rural town into a thriving metropolis. By 1890, the population had passed 50,000. It multiplied tenfold in the next three decades, surpassing 500,000 by 1920. This huge increase was largely due to migration; at no time during these years did native Californians comprise more than about one quarter of the inhabitants.[1]

At first glance, this massive migration appears perplexing. Los Angeles did not offer the traditional inducements to city building. There was no bay or natural harbor, no abundance of coal, iron, or timber to facilitate the creation of factories, and no major enterprise that stimulated the rapid flow of migrants into the town. Yet Los Angeles grew as fast as the industrializing eastern cities of the nineteenth century. Without any major manufacturing incentives, what features attracted settlers? In 1886, the California labor commissioner noted that "property, not factories, intrigued the newcomers. There are more real estate agents to the square yard than can be found in any city of the world." Indeed, by 1915 a local banker noted that "the most conspicuous fact about Los Angeles lies in it being a residential, and not an industrial community."[2]

Aside from the attractions of abundant land and mild climate, railroad and realty promoters, along with the chamber of commerce, waged a vigorous campaign to lure settlers to Los

Angeles. The rapid growth of the city continued even after the land boom. Population increase far exceeded industrial growth; most residents engaged in professions, in business, or in clerical and service jobs rather than factory work. Although local boosters claimed that Los Angeles was the "best advertised city in America,"[3] that stimulation alone cannot account for the fact that within a few decades it became one of the largest cities in the country. Who flocked to this new western city, and why did they come?

Beginning in the 1870s, native-born Americans began streaming toward the Pacific. By 1910, fully 60 percent of the California population came from the Middle West, and most of these migrants settled in Los Angeles. The early boom-town ruffians and speculators were quickly outnumbered by a flood of older, more affluent, and more pious Protestants. Bringing their families and Victorian traditions, they established churches that were to provide the bases for the city's leadership. These neighborhood congregations comprised the Protestant elite of the growing metropolis, where political and economic power were combined.[4] This consolidated local control was possible because Los Angeles was more homogeneous than most eastern cities, with their large immigrant populations. Native Americans outnumbered the foreign-born by nearly four to one in Los Angeles (see table 3). Thus the indigenous Mexicans, along with other scattered ethnic groups, were powerless against the Anglo-Saxons who migrated from the East.

A combination of attributes made Los Angeles attractive to these Protestant settlers: abundant space, few immigrants, and virtually no barriers to prevent them from taking over local leadership and building a family-centered voluntaristic community. The mild climate and lush landscape inspired enthusiastic testimonials from delighed settlers; but they never lost sight of the purposes motivating their civic life. Typical is this glowing report of the Illinois Association of Los Angeles in 1886:

Resolved: That in this grand country we have the tallest mountains, the biggest trees, the crookedest railroads, the driest rivers, the loveliest flowers, the smoothest ocean, the finest fruits, the mildest lives, the softest breezes, the purest

air, the heaviest pumpkins, the best schools, the most numerous stars, the most bashful real estate agents, the brightest
skies, and the most genial sunshine to be found anywhere in
the United States. . . . We heartily welcome other ref-
ugees . . . to make them realize that they are sojourning in a
City of the Angels, where their hearts will be irrigated by the
healing waters flowing from the perennial fountains of
health, happiness, and longevity.[5]

The above resolution reflects a combination of concerns
which occupied the early settlers: visions of paradise tempered
with pragmatic notions about schools, transportation, and real
estate. Clearly, these Midwesterners wanted something new,
fresh, and exciting. But they also wanted a place where they
could live, work, and establish families in tune with the values
of the past. Speaking of the desire of southern Californians for
an Italian-style Eden, Carey McWilliams described their aspirations well: "They wanted an Italy nearer home, an Italy
without Italians, an Italy in which they could feel at home, an
Italy in which, perhaps, they might settle and live out their days
in the sun."[6] Los Angeles attracted them with much of the old
frontier appeal: it held the potential for something different.
Because southern California was still relatively undeveloped,
they saw a unique opportunity to shape the environment according to their liking. Combining reverence for the old with
eagerness for the new, they helped set the tone for America's
first truly twentieth-century city.

Desires for newness, however, were contained within a
strong adherence to tradition; the mold in which these settlers
cast their new city was distinctly Victorian. Civic leaders did
not see their task as one of paving the way for a monumental
break from the past. Rather, they believed that cities in the
East were faced with evils that threatened community order,
along with its central foundation, the home. Therefore, they
set about their task of city building with the hope of fitting life
in this exotic Mediterranean setting into their cherished communal ethics.

The first task was to insure the survival of their system of
values. Protestant reformers in Los Angeles were well aware
that not everyone in the city shared their cultural traditions.
They were also very concerned about the problems that

plagued industrial centers of the East, and did their best to avoid them in Los Angeles. Already they had the advantage of no crowded manufacturing center in their midst. But this was no guarantee against vice in the public sphere, and they began a compaign to clean up the city.

During the late nineteenth century moral reform was beginning to influence local politics throughout the nation. Los Angeles was no exception. Because of the increasing strength of the Protestant migrants, vice districts flourished only briefly. By the turn of the century, local ordinances had limited saloons to two hundred and closed them on Sundays, outlawed gambling, shut down the vice district, suppressed prostitution, raised the age of consent, and criminalized fornication.[7] In contrast to many eastern cities still under machine control, the Progressives who accomplished these measures in Los Angeles were to dominate the social and political institutions of the city for two decades. All in all, these civic leaders were successful in placing the stamp of Victorianism firmly upon their adopted community. As one resident proudly proclaimed, "A century ago this was the Land of Mañana. Today it is the city of the strenuous life."[8]

Civic leaders in Los Angeles could insist upon conformity to the Victorian code in the public arena through local ordinances and laws. But the private realm was much more difficult to control. In spite of their confidence and optimism, signs of restlessness appeared within the genteel community. One of the most troubling was the increase in marital breakdown, signaling that serious tensions lay beneath the placid Victorian surface. Most disturbing was the fact that divorce was not concentrated among outsiders—ethnics, immigrants, or poor. Rather, it was native Protestant Americans, like those who migrated to Los Angeles, whose marriages were most likely to fall apart (see table 3).

What did domestic strife look like in a Victorian setting? First of all, it is important to keep in mind that divorce was uncommon in the nineteenth century, in Los Angeles as elsewhere in the country. During the 1880s, although marital breakdown was increasing, it had not yet become a problem of major proportions. Familial and communal ethics still held strong. Only flagrant violations of the Victorian code prompted aggrieved men and women to take their spouses to court. Sex-role expectations were clearly defined—everyone knew how a good wife should behave and what a good husband should do. Serious deviations from these basic obligations could lead to domestic upheaval. Yet rare as it was, divorce was noticeable enough to generate concern. It seemed that Victorians were finding it increasingly difficult to abide by their own code.

The marital conflicts that surfaced in the courts of Los Angeles in the 1880s reveal the fundamental principles upon which nineteenth-century marriages rested. Men and women had specific duties and lived with concrete restraints on their behavior and demeanor. Husbands were expected above all to provide adequate support for their families. In the 1880s, there was almost no controversy over what constituted the necessities of life. If the man did not supply the means for adequate food, clothing, and shelter for his family to live comfortably, his wife was entitled to a divorce. No husband questioned that; and no quarrels ensued over what his obligation entailed. One typical case was that of Martha and Everett Hickey. They were married in 1882, at Virginia City, Nevada. During their three-year marriage, which produced a single child, they moved to Los Angeles, where Everett worked as a teamster. Their property consisted of a small amount of household furniture worth $100. The basic problem in the marriage was Everett's inability to fulfill his role as provider. When Martha requested money for "the necessities of life for herself and little child, her husband, disregarding his duties as a husband toward the wife, cruelly told her that he would not give her a dollar... if she did not like it, she could leave him and go elsewhere." To make matters worse, his behavior was hardly genteel; he swore often, calling her a "lying bitch" and a "bastard." As she was a "weak, frail woman," his behavior seriously impaired her health.[9] In a similar case, Christina Arnold claimed that her husband, a miner, "never earned one cent," never provided for her, and told her, "You don't know enough to spend money. You don't know enough to buy your own clothes." To add to his other insults, when she requested two dollars for shopping, he replied, "I will shit you two dollars."[10]

Divorcing wives in the 1880s also complained if their mates' neglect forced them into the work force. This was something deplored by men and women alike. Even though nineteenth-century feminists had argued that "disease, depression, moral idiocy, or inertia, follow on an idle life,"[11] few Victorians advocated work for women. Hostility to female employment surfaced in the divorce sample. These cases reveal little controversy over whether or not a woman should work; if she had to, she did. Working wives comprised one-third of the women in the 1880s sample. This is a rather large proportion, since less than one-fourth of the entire adult female population, including single women, held jobs (see table 6). Not one wife indicated any reason for working other than sheer necessity. Thirty of the 167 working women insisted that they did not want to work at all (see table 7).

Jane Austin, for example, worked because her husband Charles never supported her and her two children. He "compelled her to earn most of the clothes which she and their children wear, from the fruits of her own labor, although her husband is an able-bodied man . . . amply able to support his family."[12] Similarly, Joseph Norton, a teamster, "never provided any reasonable or fit place or mode of living" for his wife Melvina, and she was "compelled to do hard work and drudgery for another family for board and lodging" which was "grossly unfit for her."[13] If we consider the types of jobs most of these early divorcing women held, it is not surprising to find little enthusiasm for their work. Only 8 percent held high white-collar jobs, as compared to 14 percent of the working women in the city. Moreover, nearly half worked in low-blue-collar occupations, usually as domestics or menials (see table 8). We have no evidence that any of the early divorce litigants, husbands or wives, believed in principle that a wife should work.

A husband, however, was expected to do more than merely provide the necessities of life and maintain his wife at home, out of the work force. He had to exhibit genteel behavior, tame his lusts, and protect the purity of his spouse. It was not simply for the benefit of pure womanhood; men were to avoid indulgence because it "diverts the human mind from the pursuit of well-being and disturbs the internal order of domestic life which is so necessary to success in business."[14] Restraint was

important, for the sake of the men themselves and their ability
to function in the economy. At the same time, it guaranteed
their role as provider and producer, contributing to domestic
harmony as well as national progress. Personal ethics, then,
were a central part of communal values. Because of this code,
not only vices but all sorts of amusements had to be rigorously
controlled.

There was, however, a double standard concerning the
matter of entertainment. A certain amount of indulgence was
condoned for men, who were considered to be baser creatures
by nature. Given this assumption, it is not surprising to find
that throughout most of the nineteenth century, public amusements were geared primarily to men. Although urged to behave
with restraint, men were allowed and expected to gather for a
drink at the local tavern now and then, or play cards, gamble,
or game together in various known amusement centers. In
these places, respectable women were never seen; and men of
all classes might indulge their vices in ways acknowledged—if
not openly approved—by the society. Even a certain amount
of philandering with prostitutes was tolerated for those males
whose passions could not be held in check through willpower.
Many even believed that these outlets were necessary to protect pure wives and sweethearts from dangerous lusts. Such
activities may have been frowned upon, but they were known
to exist, and accepted. As long as men indulged their vile natures in a place apart from their economic and domestic concerns, communal values would not be violated, and social life
might still conform to the Victorian code.

The case was different for women. So sharp was the distinction between "good girls" and "bad girls" that a woman who
appeared in a vice zone might ruin her reputation permanently.
Most public amusements were segregated by sex or class or
both. Middle-class men and women might attend theater or
concerts together, or private dances and balls. But there were
very few arenas where all classes and sexes mingled. The genteel community had to be protected from the taint of vice at all
cost.[15]

This segregation of amusements is revealed dramatically in
the 1880s divorce cases. Nearly every conflict that revolved
around leisure activities and entertainments implicated the

husband. It was not that these men dabbled in amusements now and then. Rather, problems began when they brought their vices home, polluting the tranquil environment. Drinking, gambling, or carousing disrupted domestic life. Either the husband squandered his money and deprived his family of basic needs, or he became violent, abusive, or irresponsible as a result of his moral lapses. Often his behavior had even more direct results, as when promiscuous men infected their wives with venereal disease. These problems all appeared in the cases; but the most common of all was vile behavior resulting from drink (see table 9).

In California, habitual intemperance was a legal ground for divorce, and it was a fairly common charge among Los Angeles couples divorcing in the 1880s. A female drunkard was even more loathsome than a man, since women were supposedly more virtuous to begin with. There were some cases of intoxicated wives in the 1880s sample, but they were rare compared to the cases indicting men for this conduct. One characteristic case involved accusations on both sides. Jonathan Jones sued his wife Sharon for divorce on the grounds of cruelty, claiming that she was "addicted to drinking" and neglected her household chores as a result. The pair had married in San Francisco in 1871 and lived together for eleven years, with no children. According to Sharon's testimony, Jonathan had a "lucrative profession" including several business interests, while she had "no means," was "feeble, almost blind, and unable to work." Both, however, seemed to own a good deal of property, including several lots of real estate each. Jonathan claimed that Sharon went out in the street barefoot in a nightdress, and was arrested for indecent exposure. He said that often when they were out, he had to take his alcholic wife home to avoid scandal.

But Sharon had a different story. She complained about Jonathan's "drunken orgies" and his neglect, which forced her on the charity of friends. She said her husband, not she, was the drunkard, and related one incident in order to dramatize her charge:

Jonathan came home one night and foamed at the mouth; and his eyes, diffused with blood, glared with the fire of untamed ferocity . . . he shrieked out a command to her to bring the chamber pot. She hastened to do so, handed him one; in consequence of his excited condition he was unable to relieve his bladder... frenzy added to frenzy... with the strength of madness he hurled the vessel at her head.

Sharon survived the attack, but said that her husband did not sober up for five days. His drinking made him violent, and he often hit and kicked her. It also unleashed his lust, for he visited brothels and wrote "lascivious, lecherous, libidinous letters" to another woman. Sharon denied all of Jonathan's charges against her, saying that she was out in her nightdress only because she had to fetch her drunken spouse. She concluded by remarking that her husband was unable to perform his responsibilities as a decent and productive husband due to his drinking. She claimed that for the last two years of their life together, Jonathan had "not been sober for ten consecutive days to have any moral impulse." The court found Sharon's allegations to be true and her husband's false, and she was granted the divorce.[16]

It is interesting to note that in these early cases, accused wives often defended themselves by arguing that their actions were motivated by proper notions of duty. Sharon Jones claimed that her seemingly inappropriate conduct was due to her efforts to "rescue" her husband from his vices. The divorce of Abraham and Laura Small is another case in point. The couple married in San Francisco in 1880, and had two children. During their stormy marriage they had frequent quarrels. Finally in 1885 Abraham, a carpenter, filed for divorce on the grounds of cruelty. His wife subsequently filed a cross-complaint, charging her husband with cruelty and adultery. Included in the file were several letters from Abraham to Laura. The early ones were friendly, although rather detached and cool. He had gone to Los Angeles looking for work, while she remained in San Francisco. Nearly all of his letters said that he would send her money as soon as he could, but he was still out of work. They began "Mrs. Small Dear Wife," or "Mrs. Small Dear Madam," and ended with messages such as, "I hope this letter finds you all well, kiss the children for me from your husband A. Small."

Abraham's letters gradually began to show signs of bitterness: "You wish me bad luck and I have not had a day's luck since I have been here but I wish you all the luck that you can have and I don't hope that you will die like a dog as you wish me." Finally he announced that he would not return to her, although he would send money for her and the children. When their case finally landed in court, fierce accusations erupted on both sides. Abraham claimed that his wife did not behave properly. She slapped him in public, threatened to kill him, and said that his mother and sister were "whores." She also swore, and associated with a "lewd" woman named Marie. Moreover, she went to saloons where she drank absinthe and came home intoxicated.

In her reply, Laura denied everything, saying that she was merely trying to implore her husband to act decently. She said that he left her for several months in San Francisco when she was sick and confined to her bed in childbirth. She admitted slapping him in public, saying that she had done it because of his "refusal to protect her from the abuse of his friend . . . who abused and called her vile names. . . . She demanded her husband's protection, but when he attempted to leave the house with his friend, refusing to afford her the protection she demanded . . . she attempted to take his hat to keep him from going . . . and acting under the impulse of the moment and suffering in mind from the insults and abuse . . . she did slap him." But she claimed he forgave her. Furthermore, Marie was introduced to her by her husband as his friend's wife. As to her drinking, she protested that the only reason she ever set foot in a saloon was "to rescue Abraham and take him home, to rescue him from his evil habits . . . believing it to be her duty as his wife to make every effort in her power."

In this case, when the husband charged his wife with uncouth, violent, and immoral conduct, she replied by stating that her actions were motivated by her desire to be protected, and her sense of duty to rescue Abraham from degeneracy. But the court remained skeptical. It did her case no good when her friend Marie was found to be a former prostitute, living in concubinage. Even if she was the "wife" of Abraham's friend, Laura's association with her was inappropiate. Clearly the double standard was at work here, for the court declared that Laura's charges against her husband were false. Although he did occasionally drink and gamble, the court determined that Abraham's inclinations were not "habits." Moderate indulgence in these activities was condoned, but only for men. Laura's conduct, however, was intolerable—whether in moderation or not. Abraham was granted the divorce, but his wife retained custody of the children, plus fifteen dollars a month for their care.[17]

Efforts to rescue husbands from their own bad habits usually were not welcomed by the errant spouse. Samuel B. Arthur was one such husband. He and Christina married in Santa Monica in 1881, when he was forty-one and she twenty-two. They lived together for a year and had no children. Christina claimed that her husband did not work and spent all his money gambling. He had a "wild, ferocious and terrible temper," tore up the house, and threatened her. But Samuel did not appreciate his wife's interfering with his freedom to indulge in leisure pursuits of his choice:

You was no lady to go for me when I was gambling up there, and bring me home, I won't walk a chalk line for any woman—I'll be damned if I'll do it. . . . You can go to hell and get a divorce if you want to . . . you are no lady, you was never raised, you was never brought up, and you are nothing. . . . I picked you up and no other man would do as I have done. . . . I will see you scrubbing floors yet for a living. . . . I'll make it damned hot for you. . . . I am a G.D.S.O.B. for living with you so long as I have.[18]

This husband, along with several others in the sample, enjoyed deviating from the genteel code. Nevertheless, that was a man's prerogative; he wanted a "lady" for a wife.

The above cases suggest a general trend characteristic of the 1880s divorces. A certain amount of male indulgence was condoned, unless the husband clearly overstepped the bounds of discretion and infused the domestic sphere with his vices. Perhaps the worst vice a man could bring home was unrestrained lust. It was considered a heinous offense if a husband unleashed his unbridled passions directly upon his wife, with no concern for her delicacy. Sexual brutality was considered a vicious crime, especially among Victorians who advocated moderation in matters of conjugal intercourse. Nearly every case in the 1880s sample that included sexual conflicts revolved around the wife's charge of her mate's abusive conduct.

Typical was the case of Mamie and Hialmer Grover. This Victorian couple married in Los Angeles in 1882, both Protestant migrants from the Middle West with native-born parents. Hialmer was a thirty-eight-year-old real estate broker, with a good deal of property and valuable possessions. Mamie was a young girl when they married. She complained that her husband was "possessed of a gross, brutal and lustful nature, which he does not control." Her affidavit explained that Mamie at the time of their marriage "was of the tender age of seventeeñ, and not a fully matured and developed woman. That commencing with the night of their marriage, the husband compelled her almost nightly to have sexual intercourse with him, and frequently as often as two to three times a night and during her menstrual periods. Frequently, he would awaken her out of her sleep and compel her to submit to his lusts. The unnatural excesses caused her health to break, and she became a frail and sickly woman therefrom." However uncouth Hialmer's private behavior, he demanded the utmost decorum from his wife. Whenever she went "out into society," he accused her of improper conduct should she "manifest any polite attention" toward his friends. He became furious when, upon his refusal to accompany her to a church social, she went by herself. He also had a vile habit of deserting her on the street after evening church services, leaving her "wholly unattended for a long space of time," to her "annoyance, mortification and fear."

Hialmer Grover demanded that his wife behave like a modest and genteel woman. But according to Mamie, he did not treat her in a manner befitting a pure and chaste wife. She expected physical protection, a social escort, and sexual restraint on the part of her spouse. Hialmer, in turn, denied Mamie's charges. Claiming that he was in poor health since his marriage, he explained that "sexual connection with his wife has been extremely infrequent and not such as to in any manner injure her health." Nevertheless, Mamie won her suit after three years of what she believed to be an intolerable marriage, with $60 per month alimony plus $100 attorney's fees. There were no children, and except for the alimony, Hialmer kept the property.[19]

The Grover case reflects a number of issues that were raised by other divorcing spouses in the 1880s. In litigations involving sexual problems, almost all of the wives argued that their husbands' lust had impaired their health. Melvina Harris was another woman who felt abused. She had also married young—age sixteen—to a twenty-seven-year-old railroad ticket agent. This Protestant couple lived together only five months. According to Melvina, her husband Joseph, "with more than brutal violence and indecency used her person to satiate his lust. That during the whole of said five months he had sexual intercourse with her every day not less than twice, and as often as six times each day—and during all of her periods of menstrual discharges during said time, he did with force and violence and with indecent frequency have sexual connection with her against her protests ... with beastly indifference to her feelings and cries of pain did hurt and injure her and seriously impair her health." She also said he never provided her with the necessities of life, and compelled her to do housework in their boarding house. His abuse and lust resulted in various disorders of the womb, and destroyed her previously good health and sound body.

Joseph Harris's defense was somewhat different from that of Hialmer Grover. He claimed, first of all, that Melvina deserted him not because of his "lascivious nature" but because he had "not provided her with some things which he had promised her at the time of their marriage, that she had been promised a buggy or an organ." Furthermore, he claimed that she "was always willing to yield to his embrace and to have sexual intercourse with him, and indeed has more than once complained to him that he was physically and sexually 'not enough for her.'" As to her "female diseases," he claimed that they were due to drugs she took to prevent pregnancy, not the result of his demands. Melvina's charges were typical of other wives; but Joseph's were unique in the 1880s sample. Apparently, the implication that his wife was not so pristine, plus his suggestion of her materialistic aspirations, and the further accusation that she took "drugs and poisons" to prevent motherhood, convinced the court of his innocence. Joseph was granted the divorce, and Melvina regained her maiden name.[20]

"Female diseases," often vaguely defined, appeared in several 1880s cases where women claimed that their husbands' sexual appetites caused them to become "frail and sickly."[21] One of these wives complained that during her four years of

marriage she was "forced to have sexual intercourse often
three times a night," and that her husband was guilty of
"habitual wanton, cruel and inhuman abuse of his marital
rights." She entreated him to "control his lustful desires"
within "reason and moderation." Her physician informed her
that she suffered from a "womb complaint of a serious
character" and told her to refrain from frequent sexual intercourse. But her husband continued his "unnatural excesses."
Apparently this wife was "frequently for weeks at a time obliged to wear mechanical appliances to keep her parts in place,
but even while so wearing such appliances he would force her
to submit to the gratification of his lusts." The physician involved seemed to be as obtuse about his diagnosis as he was
about his therapy. When asked by the court what may have
caused her various disorders, he replied, "Too violent exercise
as horseback riding, long continuous use of sewing machine,
exposure to cold and moisture, a sudden arrest of the menstrual
flow, etc." Although this woman may have been victimized by
her gynecologist more than her spouse, she was granted the
divorce and restored to her maiden name.[22]

Sexual complaints generally drew a favorable verdict from
the court; few men charged with conjugal brutality contested
the case. Only one man in the 1880s sample whose wife complained of sexual abuse defended his actions as perfectly reasonable. But his justification was hardly reassuring to his wife:
"He would not give two cents and a half for a wife like her who
did not give a man all he wanted.... It did not seem to hurt
whores to be treated in that way, and he did not see why it
should hurt his wife."[23]

As the above cases suggest, the demand for sexual gratification on the part of wives did not surface in the 1880s proceedings. Women complained of sexual abuse, not frustration.
Only two wives in the 1880s sample mentioned their husbands'
lack of sexual attention. But it was affection and procreation
they missed, rather than physical pleasure per se. One simply
claimed that her spouse was "cold, neglectful and in-
different... [that] he did not love her as a husband should love
his wife," and that he refused to share a bed with her.[24] The
other wife explained that immediately after marrying her clerk
husband, she "discovered that he was physically incapable of
entering into the marriage state, was impotent, and without

passion and incapable of having connection with a woman."
She described herself as a "young and healthy woman, amor-
ous, and passionately fond of children and the physical incapacity of the husband is a source of great annoyance and
mental suffering, that one of the principal inducements to her
to enter into the contract of marriage with him was her love for
children and her desire to have children." This wife, admitting
her passionate nature, stressed more heavily her instincts of
motherhood.[25]

In contrast to the two cases above, ten men complained that
their wives refused to fulfill the sexual side of the marital cov-
enant. Four of these husbands claimed that "without reasonable cause or justification" the wife denied them "the
privileges of a husband."[26] One of the accused wives denied
the charges, saying she "always consented to have reasonable
matrimonial intercourse whenever well and able to do so,"
although her reply betrays a certain lack of enthusiasm.[27]
Another husband was so thwarted in his efforts to gain his
wife's sexual favors that his brother-in-law told him, "Your
wife wears the breeches, and you will have to leave."[28] Jan
Morr refused sex because she "did not care to have any more
children." A witness, scornful of this woman's attitude toward
procreation, remarked that "there are not many women so
strong and rugged as she is." The husband was granted the
divorce.[29]

The remaining six husbands who complained of their wives'
incapacity claimed that it was due to some ailment, usually
"female diseases," which were very common in the nineteenth
century. In one case it was the frail wife who was granted the
divorce. Along with her husband's threats and cruelty, including his promise to "smash her head as flat as a pancake,"
he was insensitive to her physical problem. He told her that
"he could get plenty of women who were better than she was
to sleep with, that he knew she was sickly and that her condition was such that he was unable to have sexual intercourse
and co-habit with her as man and wife." Nevertheless, the
couple had four children during their sixteen-year marriage.[30]

Similarly frustrated was Randolph Kirkland, who married
Elizabeth after the mother of his four children died. Although
he remained with his second spouse for twenty years, this
minister of the gospel explained that she was "physically

incapable of entering into the marriage state . . . not competent
or in a fit condition to marry . . . that she fraudulently concealed
from him her real condition." Her disease also "rendered
cohabitation with him very offensive and injurious to his
health." Yet she refused to submit to a medical examination or
treatment to cure her "infirmity and sexual incapacity." Finally "her uterus became in a measure permanently closed and
she became wholly incapable of having any sexual intercourse
whatsoever." The husband's thirty-one-year-old daughter explained why her father tolerated this situation for so long. He
was a "quiet, peace-loving man, preferring to suffer in silence
rather than resent an injury." He was a "man of few
words . . . reticent concerning his private affairs, even to his
children." Finally this minister, who always "commanded
universal respect," divorced his second wife.[31]

These cases document the pattern of sexual complaints in
the 1880s sample. Gratification was important for men, not
women; delicacy and moderation were required for wives.
None of the proceedings suggest any concern for female sexual
fulfillment, except for the two wives whose desires for affection and children were frustrated. This was in keeping with the
Victorian code. As Tocqueville noted in the 1830s, American
marriage demanded of women "a constant sacrifice of her
pleasures to her duties," so that the home would remain well
disciplined.[32] Personal satisfaction, indeed happiness itself,
was to be derived from the fulfillment of one's responsibilities
to God, the community, and the family. No doubt that is why
women victimized by dissolute men were entitled to a divorce.
But those wives who treaded even slightly upon off-limits ter-
ritories were deemed unworthy of sympathy. If we look at the
cases filed by husbands against their wives, we find that men
complained if women deviated from the code of pure womanhood. Laziness, refusal to fulfill domestic responsibilities,
lack of subordination, or self-indulgence was not to be tolerated.

Perhaps the most grievous violation of the role of wife was
denial of motherhood. Women who were not maternal were
freaks; and no man was to be compelled to live with such a
spouse. In the 1880s, the issue rarely came up. When it did,
there was no question about the outcome. Anna Klaff, for
example, was deemed unfit as both a wife and mother. She was

married in 1880 at the age of nineteen to a twenty-three-year-old barkeeper. Three years later her husband asserted that she had gone off to Santa Monica "and there spent the day, leaving their nursing baby entirely alone and uncared for in a room in a hotel." She had given the infant drugs for sleeping. John Klaff was granted a divorce without further ado, and also gained custody of the child.[33]

More common if less serious were cases filed against women who failed to fulfill their domestic responsibilities. Emma Hearst, for example, "refused to cook the meals, make the beds, and wash the clothes." Her husband Franklin was unable to keep a farm hand, since his wife did not cook their breakfast until after 10:00. Emma made it impossible for him to conduct his other business as a tailor; and he was granted a divorce on the grounds of cruelty.[34] In a similar case, Henry Glass, a bookbinder, divorced his wife Lydia because she "refused to perform her household duties in a proper or efficient manner, including her failure to take proper care of the children." Although she "enjoys good health," she stayed in bed until 9:00 every morning.[35]

Included in the code of proper wifely conduct was subordination to one's husband, which included submerging her wishes in his. This is revealed dramatically in the case of Henry and Emily Burr. Henry was a somewhat tolerant husband married to a rather strong-willed wife, who made periodic efforts to contain her rebellious spirit. This troubled pair's strife began early, and continued throughout their fifteen years of marriage. In 1872, Emily went to Europe, leaving Henry tending his business as well as their two children. Although he gave her permission for the trip, he was not altogether happy about it, as his letters suggest:

My confidence in your fidelity is founded on a rock. I can trust you, and I was willing to give up all pleasure for myself this summer that you might have your fill. You went away with the modest request that I should take care of the children, repair the house and buy a new one, move into it, get settled and established before your return . . . if I do this my leisure moments will be all occupied. . . . Yours with the mercury at 92, Henry.

In another taunting letter, Henry expressed even more resentment, saying he was going to the "Grand Ball in a fancy suit.... I regret that you will not be permitted to look upon my loveliness, to look at me you would never suspect that I had children in rags at home or were living in a tenement home or had a wife in foreign lands, wasting her substance in riotous living."

By 1880, Henry had left, and Emily was clearly torn by remorse. In a remarkable letter, she admitted that she had not acted as a proper wife ought to, and promised to be more submissive in the future if only he would come back. She did not mention her European adventures. But she did allude to several other incidents suggesting that she was strong-minded, willful, and not as obedient as he would have liked:

My dear Henry ... I must tell you that I love you with my whole heart more than I ever loved you before.... Your boys need you.... I will not cross your *will* again, unless it be very wrong.... I have been unreasonably willful many times ... but don't let me stand in the way of my boys' interest. I am sorry I did not give you the key because you had a right to lock your door ... forgive and forget.... I feel so penitent tonight that I only think of what I have done to irritate you. I have been too impulsive but one kind word would have won me over.... I have been foolish but if you come back I will be wiser—Emmie. May God and the good angels influence you right.

Yet even in this letter, we perceive thinly veiled chastisement of her overbearing husband. She agreed never to cross his will again—unless "it be very wrong." And she further implied that her "impulsiveness" was due to his lack of even "one kind word." Whatever the immediate effect of the letter, it had no long-term palliative power. Henry was granted a divorce in 1886, denouncing Emily's "devilish actions in days gone by.... I shall never marry again. I have had quite enough of married life."[36]

The complex and bitter case of the Burrs reveals a number of themes typical of these early cases. The references to leisure pursuits outside the home fall into a Victorian mold, revolving around private parties and foreign travel. And the wife's not-so-subtle chafing at the bit, as well as her guilt and remorse about not being properly submissive, also attest to the fact that both spouses were deeply tied to traditional mores surrounding the Victorian home, although they apparently had a difficult time abiding by them. Neither spouse admitted to having abandoned these mores altogether. But it was the very efforts to conform to the code that caused friction, especially for Emily who, despite her freedom to travel in Europe, felt tyrannized by an overbearing husband who went so far as to lock her out of "his" room.

Emily Burr made efforts to measure up to standards of propriety—although she was obviously restless. Other women did not even make the effort, and indulged in activities that were totally outside the limits of respectability. Lulu Gilman, for example, was guilty of "attending public places of amusement . . . and remaining there til a late hour of the night." Marcus Gilman, a twenty-two-year-old clerk, had married eighteen-year-old Lulu in 1873 in Los Angeles. They had one child. Eight years later Marcus divorced Lulu, on the grounds of cruelty, claiming that she neglected her domestic duties owing to "idleness, frivolity and dissipation." Lulu also refused to care for their child, and used "vulgar and profane language not proper herein to be stated." She "disregarded and treated with contempt his rightful authority as her husband and against his wishes and earnest protestations has frequently deserted her home and family and gone off alone to parties, balls, and other places of amusement there to associate with and enjoy the society of other men." After his ten hours of daily labor he "frequently upon coming home at night exhausted with his daily toil, has found his home and child deserted by his wife who has often remained absent . . . a great part of the night. . . . He has been compelled to cook his own food and to nurse and care for his child at all hours of the night." Lulu's actions brought public scandal, for it was "believed by a large number of his neighbors, friends, and acquaintances that she is an unchaste woman" with "a bad reputation for chastity." His shame and mortification made him unfit for his work, and he was granted the divorce.[37]

Lulu Gilman went out unchaperoned to parties and dances, causing a public scandal. She indulged in amusements that were improper for a lady, and mingled with men in forbidden places. As a result, she neglected her domestic duties, and her morality was immediately implicated. Whereas Lulu Gilman seemed to flaunt her outrageous behavior, other women with similar inclinations for excitement tried to conceal their activities. One such wife was Ada Thayer, who married in Los Angeles in 1879, and was divorced three years later. Fred

Thayer, a railroad locomotive engineer, discovered Ada in an
opium den "kept by Chinese in what is known as Chinatown,"
and he caught her with another man "engaged in the vile habit
of opium smoking." Ada's "cruel and inhuman acts and her
language have rendered him miserable," and Fred was granted
the divorce.[38] These sorts of revelations were relatively rare.
But they do suggest that some women, like men, indulged in
vices outside the home. But unlike the men, they were condemned for it.

If a woman totally overstepped the bounds of propriety, she
became a "whore" in the eyes of her husband. This epithet
applied to wives whose behavior crossed the line between
proper and disgraceful. In the 1880s, women who were not
paragons of virtue were likely to be deemed "whores." The
charge was not taken lightly, especially by wives who were
unfairly accused. Several felt that the insult itself was such a
severe affront that it provided the sole complaint for divorce.
Emily Johnson, for example, was driven to distraction by her
husband's suspicions. "When Emily would come downtown
for the purpose of attending to some business connected with
her household affairs, he would accuse her of having dodged
into the back entrances of hotels for the purpose of illicit commerce with other men." Obviously, Charles Johnson did not
like his wife going "downtown" at all. After six years of marriage and three children, Charles called Emily a "damned
whore," and she divorced him.[39] Another woman won her suit
for divorce because her husband remarked, "I will treat you
just as though you were a Chinese whore." He also said she
was a "beast," spread rumors that she was unchaste, and
ruined her reputation.[40]

There was probably no greater affront to a woman in the
1880s than calling her a whore; and courts were sympathetic to
wives whose chastity was unjustly impugned in this manner.
Eighteen-year-old Andrea Lugo fled from her twenty-nine-
year-old husband who called her a "whore, abandoned and
unprincipled woman" and ordered her to "go away and fuck
for a living."[41] Another husband asked his wife, "How many
fifty cent pieces have you made by sleeping with other
men?"[42] In a peculiar comment, Jacob Watte, a shoemaker,
told his wife of twenty-seven years and mother of his four
children, "You are the worst whore in Los Angeles, you are

whoring with everybody in Los Angeles except me."[43] In all of these cases, allegedly false charges and insults by the husbands were the only grievances mentioned to support the wives' charges of cruelty. In each instance, the wife was granted the divorce.

If it was unforgiveable merely to accuse a woman of selling her body, forcing her to do so was even worse. Only one woman in the sample complained of this supreme violation. Lizzie Sherwood was only sixteen when she married twenty-two-year-old Walter Claner. After two years she filed for divorce, claiming that he and his mother had forced her to sell sexual favors. Walter's mother, "a notoriously indecent, licentious and disreputable woman," beat her into submission, and with Walter conspired to barter away Lizzie's chastity. She was sent out into the streets to "get money" by offering "certain men strangers" sexual favors. The two also allegedly took her to "certain notorious houses of prostitution in Los Angeles and compelled her to stand around the doors and windows."[44] Lizzie was speedily granted a divorce.

Women who were abused by unwarranted defamation of their character were entitled to a divorce. But the slightest indication that a wife was indeed unchaste guaranteed a decree in the husband's favor. This was true even if the behavior in question occurred prior to the marriage. Premarital sex was so vehemently deplored that it could disrupt a marriage that was otherwise virtuous. In nearly every case where the issue came to light, it was the woman's transgression that created the problem. In the 1880s sample, four husbands mentioned loss of female chastity prior to marriage as a cause of friction. Three of these rejected their wives immediately upon discovering that their presumed virginal brides were "used." One husband, a miller, found out that his wife "was not pure before her marriage to him" and proceeded to slap, hit, and beat her, call her a bitch and a prostitute, and tell her to "go off and sleep with other men."[45] Another, a lawyer, thought that his bride was "chaste and virtuous" when they married, but later believed she deceived him "in order to wrongfully despoil him of his property."[46] In one case, it was the wife who could not tolerate the marriage, due to her shame. She had "suffered herself to be seduced and debauched" by her husband, and became pregnant before they were married. As a result, she was "scandalized in her good name and fair reputation."[47] In these cases, the women, not the men, suffered from premarital sexual encounters. The stigma followed them into wedlock, dashing their hopes for a stable and respectable married life.

Immodest or immoral behavior during marriage was also cause for divorce, even if the woman did not transgress sexually. It was enough if a wife's demeanor suggested a lack of chastity. The McGuires, for example, were married in California in 1878, and had four children during their seven-year marriage. Wilson, a laborer, sued his wife for divorce on the grounds of cruelty. He claimed that she threw things at him, including a heavy can, a stove lid, a butcher knife, and cups and saucers. She also called him a "bastard s.o.b.," and tried to choke him. Emma McGuire replied with a cross-complaint that her husband attacked her with a stick "when she was in a delicate situation," called her a "damned bitch of a whore," and said that "he had been in all the whore houses in Los Angeles and that she, the wife, was not half as good as the meanest and dirtiest whore he saw there."

Although Wilson McGuire apparently had no qualms about admitting such extensive research, it was clearly a severe affront to his wife. She may not have been the most gentle creature, but it was not likely that she was a prostitute. Nevertheless, her husband entered a letter in the file that, he claimed, proved her guilt. She had written to his mother,

... for if any poor sinner in this world repented their sins and misgivings, I have. I am determined to be a better woman. I want to be a Christian and am determined to be, but how shall I begin oh tell me. I am hungering and thirsting to know the better way. Don't think I am just saying this, for I mean every word. I can not go to my Mother and talk this way for she would only get angry. I could tell you a good deal if I could only see you and will if I live to see you.

Whatever Emma had done wrong, she certainly felt guilty about it. In spite of her cross-complaint of her husband's cruelty and adultery, Wilson was granted the divorce.[48]

If Wilson McGuire exaggerated his wife's transgressions somewhat, a few men were granted divorces because they claimed they were in fact married to prostitutes. Joseph Smyth

said his wife was a "common prostitute" who ran a house of ill
fame; and John Riley, a Baptist missionary, said his wife Eva
lived in a brothel on Los Angeles street and worked as a prostitute.[49] Both wives defaulted, and the husbands won their
suits. In another intriguing case, Felicita Degrazia sued her
husband for divorce, claiming that she was an "innocent and
unsophisticated" girl of fifteen when she married her
twenty-two-year-old boot black husband. In her charges filed a
year later, she said her husband called her a "whore" and
accused her of "whoring" with other men. Oddly enough,
when questioned, she *admitted* that his charges were true![50]
Her husband was granted the divorce.

Another husband filed for divorce, believing that he had
fairly strong evidence of his wife's profession. John Brune was
married to Anna two years, with no children, when he filed for
divorce. He was a restaurant owner who claimed that his wife
committed adultery at a house of "ill fame." A witness saw the
wife drinking wine until midnight with strange men, and then
disappear behind a closed door of a notorious hotel. She also
created a public disturbance in her husband's restaurant,
"made loud noise . . . and called him vile names and used cruel
and abusive language toward him . . . and then drew a revolver
and threatened to shoot him." In her answer, the wife denied
everything, saying she was "at all times subject to his will as a
dutiful wife." She claimed that her husband was influenced by
"vicious and designing persons," and that he gave expensive
gifts to "loose women with whom he is intimate." The husband
retorted that his wife had been infected with a loathsome disease, "the pox."

The case had an interesting resolution. The divorce was denied, for the court found that the charges on both sides were
false and that the two "behaved . . . toward each other in a
reasonably proper manner." But the wife was granted tempo-
rary alimony for the duration of the proceedings. When John
did not pay, she claimed he was in contempt of court. He
replied that his wife's conduct had hurt his business so badly
that he could not affort the payments. He said she "leased a
house in Santa Monica for the purpose of keeping a house of
prostitution" and "proclaimed herself to the world as a
whore." Witnesses said they saw men come and go from her

room, and she kept the door locked so her son could not enter. John believed that Anna had "displayed diamonds of great value to diverse persons, and has always had money in abundance . . . she would not be kept on her good behavior for the paltry sum of $75 per month, that she could make more at her business."[51]

Perhaps Anna Brune was indeed a prostitute. After all, as the common wisdom of the day would have it, society needed "bad girls" in order to protect "good girls." Prostitution may well have been a thriving business in Los Angeles in the boom-town 1880s. Perhaps women with a taste for forbidden excitements and a comfortable income turned to this age-old occupation. If it took so little to cross the line into immoral behavior, some of these wives may have opted for activities totally outside the bounds of propriety—especially if respectability appeared to be a boring row to hoe.

Whatever the reasons, we do find the issue of whoredom taken quite seriously in the 1880s. Respectable women who were accused of it felt that the smudge on their reputation and honor entitled them to a divorce. Men who suspected that their wives were either professional prostitutes or "loose women" severed their marriages. Clearly, this issue was something of an obsession—and it also may have been a reflection of reality. These were the days before the vice crusaders outlawed prostitution. By 1920, if a husband called his wife a "whore," it was almost always hurled as an epithet, rather than a genuine accusation.

The divorce cases from the 1880s in Los Angeles demonstrate that Victorian expectations surrounding marriage still held strong. Nobody believed that a woman should have a career, or be passionate and sensual. Spouses hoped their partners would make certain sacrifices, fulfill specific obligations, and conform to a pattern of behavior appropriate for maintaining a tranquil home. The bounds of decent conduct for men and women were quite strictly defined. A nonmaternal wife was condemned, as was a lazy woman who did not maintain her home and children in good order, or who was not subservient to her husband. A proper lady did not indulge in drinking or public amusements. And a woman who was unladylike or blatantly immodest was deemed a shameless hussy or a downright whore. A married man faced equally demanding sex-role prescriptions. He had to be a good provider, keep his impulses in check, protect the chastity of his wife, and avoid vices. If he indulged in activities such as drinking or philandering with prostitutes, he could not permit them to invade the respectable home and community. In his domestic and productive life, he had to be sober and restrained.

These litigations suggest that marriage was based on duties and sacrifices, not personal satisfaction. Spouses considered each other helpmates—providers and protectors of the home rather than partners in pleasure. Such obligations and qualities were important not only for the family unit, but for the entire community as well. Sex roles were defined in terms of civic goals; and the home itself functioned as an institution geared toward the public good. In Los Angeles, as we have seen, civic leaders tried to build a city that would foster virtuous home life, which would in turn create a harmonious Victorian community. Accordingly, marriage was part of an effort to establish a tranquil domestic environment. Violations of familial ethics which culminated in divorce were an affront to the community as well as the aggrieved spouse. Husbands and wives neither expected nor hoped that their spouses would provide them with ultimate fulfillment in life, or that the home would be a self-contained private domain geared toward the personal happiness of individual family members. As one Victorian described his own upbringing,

God bless our home never meant make our home a happy one. The blessing was asked upon those virtues which were often more conducive to moral conduct and material success than happiness.[52]

Although broken marriages were still relatively rare, Americans were finding it increasingly difficult to live according to the strict sex roles and communal values that defined appropriate behavior. During these years, divorce resulted from failure to live up to Victorian expectations—it did not represent a quest for something new. The complaints of these divorcing men and women indicate no yearnings to be free from the expectations of the past. Rather, it was breaches in proper conduct that led to domestic upheaval. One of the most striking features of these early litigations is the remarkable degree of agreement over what constituted correct behavior. Spouses may have quarrelled over whether or not one's conduct deviated from the norm; but the norm itself was never a source of controversy. The family remained the cornerstone of Victorian society. The culture was still integrated, public and private life were still fundamentally intertwined, and few Victorians questioned the precepts upon which they were raised. During the turn-of-the-century decades, however, much of this would change.

Three
The Home: From Sacrifice to Satisfaction

As the divorce cases from Los Angeles in the 1880s indicate, the late nineteenth century witnessed a slight straining against the limits of Victorianism. But the code itself had not yet begun to crack from within. Not until the turn of the century was there a widespread effort to reach beyond the bounds of the Victorian ethic. After 1900, the communal values of sacrifice, voluntarism, and virtuous domesticity were seriously shaken by the rise of urban culture, which brought altered sex roles and post-Victorian expectations of marriage and family life. These changes were taking place all over the country; but nowhere were they more obvious than in Los Angeles, where the residents struggled to come to terms with the upheaval taking place in their community. What was the nature of this upheaval, and how did American urbanities cope with it?

The quest for something new found its most immediate target in the home. But the change that gave rise to a new concept of family life lay in the economy, not in the domestic realm. The corporate order emerged full-blown in the early twentieth century, striking a fatal blow to the entrepreneurial ethos that had given meaning to the sex roles and communal values of America's dominant groups during the previous century. This change was readily apparent in Los Angeles, where corporate America took a firm hold, as post-Victorians tried to hold on to the traditional fusion of public and private life within their adopted city. Yet the tides of change could not be stemmed. Ironically, it was the very newness and non-industrial nature of Los Angeles that led to its eventual emergence as a pace-setting twentieth-century city. Gradually, the pillars of Victorianism began to crumble.

The first evidence of this transformation appeared in the work force. It was here that the carefully defined activities of Victorian men and women were irreversibly altered. For men, the rise of large organizations undercut the possibility for economic autonomy in the open market, long the goal of American manhood. Beginning in 1870, in the nation as a whole, the proportion of independent businessmen in urban areas declined steadily, and it became more and more difficult for a man to be self-employed. By 1910, while the population of the nation had increased two and one-half times, the "new middle class"—technicians, salaried professionals, clerical workers, sales personnel, and public service employees—had multiplied eightfold, comprising 63 percent of the entire middle class. The corporations created such a massive bureaucracy that by 1939, 1 percent of the firms in the United States employed over half the people working in business.[1] Scholars have generally agreed that this development was important, but its implications are a matter of debate. Some argue that the most profound result was the decline of personal satisfaction derived from the job, due to the monotonous routine of the corporate order. Others emphasize the new elements of structure and stability that the system provided, giving order to a previously chaotic economy.[2] Both assertions testify to the fact that the nature of work had indeed changed. For better or for worse, the entrepreneurial ethos could no longer be maintained in the midst of masive organizations.

Work changed for the laboring classes as well. The craft tradition had been declining throughout the nineteenth century, but the emphasis on time-clock routine and single-task jobs accelerated during the turn-of-the-century decades. Scientific management did for the workers much of what bureaucratization did for white-collar employees: it added routine and order, possibly decreased the amount of physical work involved in the job, and provided a modicum of stability. Obvious advantages came in the form of more money and free time, as wages rose and the work week shrank. There is no need to romanticize the nineteenth-century economy, with its ruthless competition and abominable exploitation of labor. But the corporate system did not erase all these problems. Rather than humanize the process of work, it supplied new fruits of production to absorb wages and occupy time off the job. As a result, although men of all classes continued to identify their function in life with their jobs, they began looking for new rewards in leisure.

The change for women was even more profound, in terms of both economic activity and public behavior. Between 1880 and 1920, they went to work in unprecendented numbers. While the proportion of men in the work force remained fairly stable, the proportion of women rose 50 percent. This increase was not so dramatic among working-class women, for domestic work and factory labor were not new to them. The most striking increase was among middle-class females, married as well as single. Daughters of Victorians now joined sons of entrepreneurs in the swelling white-collar ranks. Not only did this erode the traditional woman's role; it also drastically altered the tenor of the work force. No longer was the business world an all-male arena; now both men and women filed into the ordered and predictable corporate system, to work side by side.[3] Most working women were subject to the same routine as the majority of men, only they usually lacked the same possibilities for advancement, equal pay, or job alternatives. These women, probably even more than their male counterparts, looked forward to their free time, when they could reap the rewards of their work.

Both men and women, then, became preoccupied with material goods and leisure as the mature industrial economy generated abundance. Between 1897 and 1921, the net national product increased from $15.8 billion to $70.3 billion, while the per capita national product jumped from $231 to $793—a growth rate not equaled until the post–World War II period. This meant that more wealth was available on a mass level, and luxuries formerly limited to the wealthy were within the reach of the middle classes. As early as the 1890s, Thorstein Veblen noted a significant trend, most advanced in urban areas: "As increased industrial efficiency makes it possible to procure the same means of livelihood with less labour, the energies of the industrious members of the community are bent to [achieving] . . . a higher result in conspicuous expenditure." Higher wages combined with mass advertising yielded a new consumer ethic. The amount spent nationally for personal consumption nearly tripled between 1909 and 1929, with the most striking increases for clothes, personal care, furniture, mechanical appliances, cars, and recreation. Even though the nation's wealth remained unequally distributed, some of the benefits of prosperity did filter down to the working classes. Mass

consumption offered the promise—or the illusion—that the
good life was now within everyone's reach.[4]

But the rising standard of living was something of a mixed
blessing. Affluent post-Victorians may have found it difficult to
adjust to abundance. It was more than material goods that
disturbed them; much of their entire cultural tradition was
undercut by the new organizational life. Most frightening of all,
perhaps, was that corporate employees, including their own
young women, were increasingly drawn to the sorts of public
amusements that were once the despised domain of outsiders.
Now middle-class individuals, particularly youths, had the
time, money, and inclination to indulge in these pursuits. Los
Angeles was not immune to these forces, so threatening, it
seemed, to the American home. Immorality could invade the
City of the Angels as easily as other cities where Americans
were becoming restless at work and eager to partake of new
leisure adventures. This prospect was heightened in Los
Angeles, where an exotic heritage and a mild climate gave the
city the atmosphere of a resort.

Newcomers to the modern frontier flocked to pleasure zones
with great enthusiasm, giving Protestant reformers visions of
the imminent collapse of their moral universe. In response,
local citizens made strenuous efforts to combat all threats to
their community. Indeed, as late as 1916 when the non-
Progressive police chief was elected mayor of the city, the
National Municipal Review reported a general fear that an
"open town" would be inaugurated, similar to the wild days of
the land boom. "But this view failed to take into consideration
that the temper of the community will not stand for very much
latitude along these lines." The liquor business was still restricted, there was "no red-light district, no dancing in cafes,
nor any of the usual concomitants of an 'open town.'"[5] These
local ordinances were hardly unique to Los Angeles. They were
typical of Progressive reforms all over the country aimed at
minimizing the ill effects of the Victorian decline.

Yet ultimately the post-Victorian leaders of Los Angeles
realized that they could not turn back the clock. Accordingly,
they tried to make the best of the situation by incorporating the
positive elements of progress and prosperity with the cultural
values of the past. Since they could not remove the attraction
of leisure pursuits, Progressives turned to the task of reforming

and uplifting them. In this way, amusements might become safe for the entire society, and even prove to be socially constructive, recreational facilities as well. If all classes and ethnic groups were going to mingle in these leisure realms in any case, it was better to control, regulate, and utilize them for the public good than to make futile efforts at stamping them out. For example, social dancing was considered a potentially dangerous activity that might lead youth astray. But rather than close all dance halls, reformers brought them under civic control. After considerable public agitation, municipal dances were sponsored by the newly created City Mothers' Bureau, with "marvelous" results.[6] "By the establishment of social centers of this character," proclaimed the mayor, "opportunity is offered to young men and women to indulge in innocent and healthful recreation under suitable auspices."[7]

In order to sustain these sorts of institutions, the Protestant leaders of Los Angeles had to be certain that their political hegemony would not be challenged. They were well aware that some segments of the population might not share their moralizing inclinations. In keeping with their Victorian heritage, they feared the potential political power of outsiders. Accordingly, voters in Los Angeles created and perpetuated city-wide, nonpartisan elections which all but precluded the possibility of ethnic groups having an active voice in local government. In 1914, the citizens defeated a proposal to institute proportional representation, which would have given minority voters more direct control over their elected representatives.[8] Through such measures, the Protestants in Los Angeles solidified their cultural and political power. So effectively did they americanize the former pueblo that the only remaining signs of Mexican influence were immitative architecture and an annual fiesta—with an American girl as "La Reina."

In spite of fears of ethnic power, reformers maintained an optimistic faith in the potential for individual assimilation. There was no room in the melting pot for labor unions or monopolies. Both presumably thwarted the efforts of independent entrepreneurs, regardless of of ethnic background, in their striving to achieve success. Thus Progressives in Los Angeles wrested local political control from the Southern Pacific Railroad and at the same time maintained an open-shop town well into the twentieth century. They accomplished this in spite of frequent labor unrest and sporadic violence, such as the bombing of the *Los Angeles Times* building. If the moral citizen was to reign supreme, civic leaders would have to prevent the encroachment of organized power from above as well as below.[9]

While the goals of these efforts were similar to reform campaigns waged by Protestants throughout the nineteenth century, the new crusades reflected a profound shift in emphasis. Victorians often relied upon moral suasion or economic inducements to urge conformity to their code. From temperance to abolitionism, nineteenth-century reformers hoped to convince errant individuals to give up their evil ways. Internal restraints were deemed preferable to external controls. In fact, the Protestant ethic implied that self-disciplined individuals did not need legal intervention to regulate behavior. Institutional coercion was often a last resort, and it usually unleashed a storm of controversy.

In an effort to avoid the need for more extensive controls, reformers in Los Angeles hoped to strengthen home life. They believed that if the family could retain its character-building function, the moral community might be preserved. Yet they were well aware of desires for excitement surfacing in the city. While they did their best to prevent these inclinations from finding release in public, they realized that restless urges had to have some outlet. For this, they looked to the home. Clearly, these yearnings could be safely indulged under the protection of the family, rather than amid the chaos and anonymity of the urban streets. But the strict discipline of the Victorian home would not allow for any such frivolity. Obviously the nature of domestic life would have to be expanded and altered to accommodate this need. In the process, the concept of a unique domestic lifestyle gradually evolved.

The twentieth-century family must be explored here, in this lifestyle. It was indeed something new. Cultural values, nevertheless, are not abandoned overnight, and Victorianism had a powerful staying power. Without totally rejecting all the traditions of their past, modern Americans would try to create communities suited to a happy home life, and homes conducive to personal fulfillment. In Los Angeles, this concept of family life became a primary goal of urban development. The post-Victorian civic leaders did not abandon their belief in the home as the primary social institution. They still affirmed family values as the means to achieve community ends. For this reason, Los Angeles Progressives were ultimately concerned with providing an urban atmosphere conducive to domestic harmony. The essence of this philosophy was articulated by a Protestant minister turned social worker, Dana Bartlett, who was born in Maine, raised in Iowa, and came to Los Angeles as a committed social-gospel reformer. In his 1908 book *The Better City,* he asserted, "Grant perfect family life and the majority of philanthropic and reformatory institutions would close their doors."[10]

Although faith in the home held strong, the domestic environment was now cast in a new light. Of primary importance was the domicile itself, specifically the single-family dwelling. Los Angeles, Bartlett proclaimed, "shall be a city of homes, and therefore a city without slums. . . . Here will be found only healthy, happy families." This private life could best be nurtured in isolated residential neighborhoods. Ideally, the population would be

scattered over a vast area, twenty-five persons to the acre, rather than 1,000 as in the tenement districts of our larger cities. . . . The laying out of new subdivisions far out beyond the city limits makes cheap and desirable home sites obtainable for a multitude of working men, where they are able to build cheap bungalows. . . . "The family unit," the desire of the sociologist, can be recovered . . . far from the noisy city. No work in civic betterment is worth more than this.

With this notion, Bartlett and his contemporaries went about building their "better city" in suburbia.[11]

Suburbs were nothing new to America. Throughout the nineteenth century, as transportation advances made it possible to live a distance from one's place of work, residences spread out from urban centers. By the late nineteenth century, most American cities were developing suburbs at an accelerating pace.[12] During this time, suburbs came to symbolize more than merely places to live; they signaled a new lifestyle. Los Angeles did not suburbanize in the technical, legal sense. Unlike eastern cities, where settlement spilled outside municipal boundaries, suburbs in Los Angeles fell within the city

proper. Because the city emerged when technology and communication favored suburban growth, newcomers spread over
the area quickly. Without factories to cluster settlement, rail-
way companies and realtors linked outlying areas, subdivided
them, and attracted settlers. Essentially, Los Angeles suburbanized as it urbanized, becoming a city of sprawling residential communities.

By the turn of the century, the suburban lifestyle that took
shape in Los Angeles was already becoming a national
phenomenon. "The twentieth-century city is a suburbanized
city," proclaimed one contemporary writer. And Los Angeles,
having the third most rapidly growing suburban population,
was indeed a modern metropolis.[13] Attesting to the increasing
popularity of the new lifestyle, *Cosmopolitan* magazine as
early as 1903 carried a feature article entitled "Suburban Life
in America." The author asserted that the suburb offered a
"compromise for those who temper an inherent or cultivated
taste for green fields... with an unwillingness to entirely
forego the delights of urban gaiety." The writer perceived that
these were not merely realms for the wealthy elite, but that
"people of moderate means" could live there. Whatever
their social or ethnic origins, however, suburban residents
were unified and protected by their adherence to a specific
code. In this sense, the suburbs were exclusive. As *Cosmopolitan* noted,

The householder can rely upon quite a rigid enforcement of
the restrictions designed to ensure the erection in the suburb
of residences of a uniformly creditable character, and he is
protected from the encroachments of manufacturing and other
interests likely to constitute uncongenial neighbors. Saloons
and shops, also, are excluded from these *sacred* precincts.[14]

The attraction of suburban life, then, was by no means limited to Los Angeles, nor to middle-class, post-Victorian Protestants. In fact, it is an erroneous assumption that suburbs are
homogeneous, ethnically segregated, socially exclusive communities. They encouraged rather than resisted ethnic mixture.
Suburbia fit well into the melting-pot ideal; any families could
live there (except, until recently, black and Hispanic), as long
as they could pay the price and conform to the moral order.
The pluralistic society of America found its ideal locale in the

city suburbs, where various ethnic, religious, and immigrant groups collected and assimilated. These diverse communities preserved social cohesion by absorbing congenial elements and prohibiting unwelcome ones.[15] Zoning laws were instrumental in defining the restrictions and protecting the residents' private familial domains. Accordingly, "one of the distinctive attributes of Suburban life . . . is found in the social life which is thus nurtured."[16] In this sense, they served some of the same functions as the voluntary associations of the nineteenth century that gathered like-minded individuals together.

Domestic life in suburbia was not necessarily suffocating. Modern urban families could begin to enjoy a more expansive and creative existence than their Victorian forebears. Especially in a new city like Los Angeles, Americans hanging in the balance between traditional and modern mores could experiment with new-found affluence and leisure time. In neighborhoods safely removed from vice and the sordid concerns of the business world, ambivalent urbanites could explore the possibilities of a post-Victorian era, and indulge their urges for fun and excitement. With a climate conducive to relaxation, and the landscape reminiscent of its exotic Spanish heritage, Los Angeles seemed to have captured the best of both worlds. As one astute historian observed, the American middle classes had become restless, and "began to reach out for wider horizons." They had "pent-up longings for the bizarre, the novel, the exotic."[17] Los Angeles provided a safe place for these longings. It was a romantic city on the far edge of the western frontier, divided into safe, protected neighborhoods, removed from the "influx of foreigners with low ideals of family life."[18] Here even people with modest means could cultivate their private lives, fulfilling desires for excitement and indulgence without transcending moral limitations. The suburban lifestyle that flourished in this city provided urban advantages without urban problems, affluence without loss of virtue, and high-level consumption in an egalitarian environment. Ironically, however, the lifestyle generated in Los Angeles gradually eroded the communal impulses that had previously connected the home to the public arena. In this sense, although the early civic leaders were successful in achieving their immediate goals, they failed in their ultimate aims.

What the reformers in Los Angeles finally achieved was the creation of a city ideally suited to the corporate era. They had avoided organized control by monopolistic businesses and labor unions, excluded ethnic groups from political power, eliminated vice from residential areas, fostered and sponsored legitimate recreational facilities, and housed most of the city's residents in suburban single-family dwellings. Much of this would not have been possible without large-scale institutional efforts. Progressives employed legal and political controls to insure personal morality as well as fair business practices in the civic realm. As cultural reformers, they attempted to channel desires for excitement into the private sphere, which would become further isolated and protected from public life. The law was their principal tool in this effort, and they ushered in a new trend in governmental intervention that would accelerate throughout the twentieth century. Ironically, reformers created more institutions in order to cope with the ill effects of organizational life. By expanding the bureaucratic network, they fed the very monster that gave rise to their anxieties. As the governmental structure reached further into individual lives, it undercut the voluntaristic ethos the Protestants hoped to restore. Ultimately, they were fighting bigness with bigness, and generating more of the very restlessness they hoped to contain. In the midst of this process, the ideological unity between public and private life gradually disintegrated.

The changing nature of the family takes on special importance in this context. Although the nineteenth-century middle-class home did not function directly as an economic unit, the roles of household members were defined vis-a-vis the productive system. The twentieth century brought a shift in this ethos. Now the home became one of the primary places where the fruits of production would be consumed. Family members became not merely producers, but purchasers of the goods they helped to create. In order to keep the system thriving, ascetic discipline was no longer so crucial; rather, indulgence served this new economic function more efficiently. Suburban families became consuming units, absorbing abundance and leisure into the home. In this sense, although the home may have lost some of its previous social functions, it evolved into an even more important institution for satisfying personal desires.

The residents of Los Angeles could reap the rewards of the good life in isolated suburban neighborhoods. The home remained one of the few domains where individuals retained primary control over their lives. But it was a far cry from the disciplined and ascetic domicile favored by the Victorians, with its ideological connections to the public arena. In fact, the family realm gradually became one of the main places where individuals looked for fulfillment in life. If the work experience was routinized and depersonalized, and civic affairs were no longer immediately connected to domestic virtues, private life to a large extent became cut off from public concerns. With this increasing isolation, the home became a focal point for personal gratification. Accordingly, marriage—the foundation of family life—came to mean something new.

Four
The Path to Modern Marriage

The suburban lifestyle that evolved in Los Angeles became a model for the rest of the nation. Not only were other new cities developing similar patterns of residential spacing, but the style of domesticity radiating from this West Coast locale set the tone for urban living throughout the country. It is no accident that during the first two decades of the century, Los Angeles gave birth to Hollywood, center of motion picture production. Americans looked to the movies for clues on how to cope with modern life, and the Hollywood-based industry was in a particularly appropriate locale for sending out vivid images to the populace. New sexual roles, styles of courtship, and marriage itself received thorough treatment on film. Screens all over America showed anxious viewers how to live the home life that had become associated with urban culture, particularly in metropolitan centers like Los Angeles.

One of the most popular motifs in the movies revolved around modern marriage and how to achieve it. Clearly, there was something new surrounding expectations for wedded bliss; but traditional patterns were not totally discarded. Americans struggled to come to terms with modern matrimony without giving up the values and norms of the past. As couples tried to tread the fine line between the new and the old, the movies began offering ideas on how the two might be merged. The film maker who most successfully capitalized on the formula was Cecil B. DeMille, who showed the public how to combine new sexual styles and affluence with traditional virtues. In a series of extravagant films, DeMille portrayed an entirely new type of marriage. One typical example of this postwar genre, *Why Change Your Wife,* emphasized the need to enhance domesticity with excitement and allure. The husband, bored at work, looks forward to his hours off the job when he can enjoy life with his wife. But she constantly thwarts his eagerness for fun and sensuality. He invites her dancing but she prefers a concert. He buys her revealing lingerie; she rejects it as "indecent." The husband is rebuffed one more time when he telephones his wife from his singularly drab and sterile office. Just then, the model from the dress shop enters and agrees to go dancing with exasperated man. This event leads to a divorce, and the husband goes on the marry the model, Sally.

The ex-wife, overhearing some women remark that she lost her husband because she "dresses like an aunt, not his wife," decides to change her ways and "go the limit." She buys a new wardrobe of seductive clothes and takes on a flirtatious personality. Meanwhile, the husband finds that Sally wants to "play" too much, and is only after his money. Finally they divorce, as Sally comments that the "only good thing about marriage is alimony." Soon afterward, the husband meets his first wife at a fashionable resort, clad in a revealing swimsuit and surrounded by admiring men. He is attracted to her before he realizes who she is. They reunite, and the exciting style is then brought back into the moral home.

The message is clear. The man wants both excitement *and* domesticity in a wife, who can then revitalize him in the home. The first wife was initially unsatisfying because she was *too* moral. The second wife was discarded because she was *immoral*. In the end, the two qualities merge into a new style of marriage that promises to contain both elements successfully. A satisfying union has to maintain a delicate balance between old-fashioned duties and modern excitement. Only then, presumably, can the home fulfill new demands for happiness.[1]

How was this modern marriage to be achieved? The marital formulas emanating from Los Angeles fed into a new ideal captivating the imagination of America. Through all forms of media and popular culture, the Hollywood ideal was finding its way into the lives and aspirations of the population. This development occurred not only in Los Angeles, but in other urban centers as well. In their 1920s study of Muncie, Indiana, for example, Robert and Helen Lynd examined how life there had changed since the 1890s: many of their most striking observations concerned new expectations surrounding love and marriage. As private life took on expanded dimensions, young men and women looked to each other with hopes that differed from the past. The Lynds noted that Muncie's population increasingly adhered to the notion of "romantic love as the only valid basis for marriage." Prior to wedlock, both partners spent several years of adolescence geared, presumably, to preparing for the great event. As an indication of how Muncie's youth learned about matrimony, the city librarian noticed an increasing interest in "sex adventure" fiction that "centers about the idea of romance underlying the institution of marriage." Muncie's youth were assured that "love just happens . . . you'll know when the right one comes along." Yet much of their early education, both formal and informal, was geared toward "how to know." A Muncie businessman declared, "The things girls get from high school is the ability to know how to choose a 'real one' from a 'near one.' "[2] This is a remarkable observation, for it suggests that the training of young people, especially women, was ultimately geared toward the hunt for a spouse. In Muncie as well as elsewhere in the country, this emphasis on love and marriage yielded striking results: twentieth-century Americans were marrying younger, and more often, then their predecessors.[3]

How can we explain this phenomenon? We must first look to youth and the process of mate selection for clues to the rising rate of marriage and the lowering age of brides and grooms. The rituals of courtship among the young not only shed light on expectations surrounding matrimony; they also reveal crucial connections between the corporate order and the modern home. The cultivation of romance was not cheap; it required the free time and abundance that only a mature industrial system could provide. Since necessity no longer forced them to take jobs, young people could become the pioneers of a new style of romance. The economy demanded less manpower, and university education delayed entry into the work force for an increasing percentage of the middle class, stretching "youth" far beyond physical maturity. While in 1900, 62 percent of the males between fourteen and nineteen years of age were in the labor force, by 1920 their proportion had decreased to 51.5 percent.[4] As a result, a new leisure class emerged, composed of young individuals who could afford to spend their time in consumer spending and amusements.

Suppliers of consumer goods were not oblivious to this

youthful market. In the early twenties, *Photoplay* magazine
conducted a study of advertising and found that most large
department stores quite self-consciously geared their selling
efforts toward young buyers—who were the major
consumers—and to older people who wanted to stay young.[5]
Women in particular were advised to consider youthfulness the
key to happiness, and to pursue it, literally, at all costs.
Readers of magazines such as *Cosmopolitan* learned that
"Love is Youth. . . . Age is decay, while youth is hope, and
hope is the spirit of loving."[6] Given this equation, it is not
surprising that the Lynds found an increasing preoccupation
with "youthful beauty." Although romance was an intangible
quality, appearance was real enough, and the new affluent generation did not hesitate to spend some of its abundant time and
resources to beautify itself and maintain the look of youth.

Since women usually did not work and were expected to
face marriage as their major enterprise in life, they were to
invest the greatest amount of time and energy in cultivating the
youth cult. The most influential columnist to give advice to
Muncie's loverlorn, Dorothy Dix, wrote that "good looks are a
girl's trump card." She advised, "Dress well and thereby appear fifty percent better looking than you are. . . . Make yourself charming."[7] The pursuit of love and romance was to con-
sume women more than men. As one popular writer proclaimed,

Romance will be so long as the world shall last. . . . Romance
is the poetry of existence. . . . It is given to women to be the
special custodians of Romance. . . . For women and for love of
woman the World has been conquered and its wealth laid at
her feet.[8]

In pursuit of this ideal, then, women were advised to take some
of the wealth laid at their feet and use it to enhance their
powers of attraction. Not surprisingly, capitalizing on this
youth cult proved profitable. Between 1914 and 1925, the cosmetics business increased from $17 million to $141 million.
French perfumers estimated that 71 percent of American
women over eighteen used perfume, 90 percent face powder,
73 percent toilet water, and 55 percent rouge. Over 7,000 kinds
of cosmetics were on sale by 1927.[9]

Madison Avenue not only tapped the quest for youthfulness,

it contributed to expanding the demand. Marketing efforts were geared to offering purchasable solutions to personal problems. Typical was a 1921 advertisement for Woodbury skin preparation that promised a remedy for those times "When Failure Hurts the Most:"

Are you having the good times other girsl have? Or when you come home from the party where you longed to be successful, gay, triumphant—do you suffer from a feeling of disappointment—defeat?[10]

Physical trimmings, from make-up to clothes, were all geared to attracting men. One noted dress designer, who believed that "Mystery" is the "key to all that is charming... seductive...beautiful in feminine attire," added a revealing analogy:

Feminine beauty without the proper sartorial setting is like a hook without bait. A woman who is not charmingly dressed knows only half of life.[11]

Presumably, the unknown half of life would be the male half.

Youthfulness was more than a matter of appearance; it was also one of style. To be youthful meant to participate in active leisure. "Cultivate bridge and dancing, the ability to play jazz and a few outdoor sports."[12] The ideal of youth not only gave focus to the intangible quest for romance, it also helped solve a perplexing problem for the affluent generation: how to make use of abundance and free time. Beyond this, it gave new meaning to the home, which had lost many of its former social functions. The private domain of family life now broadened into a center for personal recreation. Money could be spent in buying beauty; leisure time could be occupied in cultivating style. Women, not only as the "custodians of romance" but also as the guardians of the home, were the logical ones to pursue youth and beauty most actively. By no coincidence, they also made up the majority of the nation's "leisure class" and most active consumers.

To achieve love, then, women were to devote themselves to becoming physically attractive, something that took time, money, and skill. Contemporary observers were well aware that the new "shibboleth of youth and beauty" had become a national obsession. In 1916 one writer claimed,

Never in the history of the world have fame and wealth been so lavishly heaped upon the altar of youth and beauty. It is as though beauty were weighted in the scales against talent, education, training, and even genius, and outbalanced them all in the value of public opinion and reward.[13]

The cult of youth and beauty, though integral to the "new" generation and associated with the "new" woman, did not promote women's independence or alter their stance vis-a-vis men. Rather, it represented an intensification of efforts to attract male attention. This particular kind of attraction was extremely significant, especially within the context of the youth cult and courtship. The "flapper" image stressed adolescent, childish appearance typical of the flat-chested and boyish girl. One observer perceived that "long slender limbs and an undeveloped torso are typical of immaturity . . . characteristics of the fuller figure are discountenanced. The bosom must be small and virginal, and maturity . . . is concealed as long as long as possible."[14] In other words, youthfulness may have had romantic appeal, but it was not the look of full-blown womanhood.

This childish aura suggests that even as adults, women remained in a state of dependency on men, consistent with their traditional positions in both the economy and the home. They could gain the attention of men, but not from a stance of autonomy. The apparent freedom of the flapper, then, led directly to the protective support of a man. This style was a somewhat ironic prerequisite to romance. Coquettish, yes, but seriously intimate it was not. Some contemporaries were aware of the shallowness of this youthful ideal, among them Elinor Glyn, screen writer for numerous silent films. In 1921 she wrote that there were many lovely actresses in the moving-picture world, idols of emulation for women and adoration for men. But Glyn perceived that these screen stars of idealized beauty were "all so very young! The oldest not more than twenty-five or six—so that is why all the pretty eyes have the same expression. For the eyes are the windows of the soul, and without experience of life, there must be sameness in what looks forth."[15]

More significant than her insight, however, was her solution. She did not advocate more "experience of life" for these girls, which would have given them greater depth and maturity. Nor did she suggest shifting to older actresses. Rather, she offered a "charm school...in which I could teach them how to acquire individuality and fascination and attraction."[16] This was a safe response appropriate to the emerging status quo: the institutionalization and formalization of allure into a marketable style.

The cultivation of feminine charms may have served to underscore the dependence of women on men. But it also suggested ways to gain some degree of power. As one contemporary female writer proclaimed,

Today the world is a woman's world.... She has "with bare and bloody feet climbed the steep road of wide empire," but today she stands at the top, mistress of the world. Man with his talents, his strength, and his selfishness, has been tamed to her hand. The sensual dominant brute with whom she began... stands beside her today, hat in hand, her lover-husband; tender, faithful, courteous, and indulgent.[17]

In matters of sex, marriage, and domestic life, then, a woman could be the master of her mate. But first she had to "catch" him. What did men desire in future wives, youthful beauty or domestic virtues?

According to the popular literature, the answers were not entirely clear. Even journals with the most confirmed ideological commitments were likely to confuse the issue. The highly conservative *Ladies Home Journal*, for example, polled one hundred young men, and assured its female readers that prospective husbands did not care about physical beauty or clothes, but only the attributes of good wives and mothers. Yet at the same time the *Journal* advised that "the cardinal principle of a young wife should be to keep her heart as young as possible. Then she will longest keep her own youth." Moreover, in the midst of all the pages upholding the traditions of pure womanhood were numerous advertisements telling readers how to achieve love and happiness through beauty. As early as 1901, the back cover of one issue pictured a lovely young girl picking daisies in a meadow. The message claimed:

A Maiden's Wishes
        are but three
        O'er all the world, who'ere she be—
        To handsome grow,
        And have a beau,

> And to the bridal altar go—
> All these functions of her hope
> Come Quickly If She'll
> USE PEAR'S SOAP[18]

The formula, then, was that youth and beauty would grant your wishes—and the ultimate wish was to marry.

Mass media combined with mass consumption to democratize the marriage market. Ready-made clothing and the proliferation of cosmetics made the styles of the rich available at prices the less affluent could afford, enabling young women of all classes to become "ladies." Accordingly, if style and attractiveness were the qualities men desired, then any woman could compete for any man. In the cities, with less stress placed on family background and small-town social ties, women found a wider choice of available men. Given greater marital options, hopeful brides began to desire more than merely the security of a roof over their heads. But the cult of romance included more than purchasable goods; men and women had to offer a vast array of enticements that promised a future of happiness and bliss. In fact, since women were to attain their ultimate destiny through their marital attachment, the men had to live up to extremely high expectations.

For most women, marriage essentially defined their lives. Thus suitors had to promise to satisfy their total needs and provide them with "happiness." Expounding upon the "how to" of romance, Lavinia Hart, a writer for *Cosmopolitan,* addressed herself to men. In "The Way to Win a Woman," she began,

Be worthy of her. . . . The true woman is not won by ordinary means. . . . It is not enough that he satisfy the physical and mental, though he rarely does so much, but he must reach and awake and satisfy the ethical, spiritual part of her nature—else there must be something lacking, something unfed, some little, empty void between them which constitutes a gap in the otherwise perfect understanding.

The implication was that women were incapable of fulfilling themselves; men must do it for them. And if there was any "empty void" or shred of unhappiness, the man was considerd a failure to his woman. But even satisfying all of these needs was not enough:

When the man who would win a woman is all these things, worthy and strong and sincere, honest and consistent and steadfast, he must be one thing more—a hero.[19]

The heroes, then, must not only satisfy the emotional desires of their women, but attain a proper level of worldly success. This meant maintaining a lifestyle that was both affluent an exciting. Men had to acquire personality, much as women had to cultivate good looks and the art of flirtation. Both sexes were concerned with developing outward qualities of personal charm that would serve, essentially, as bait. This pursuit took on new and urgent seriousness for men as well as women. "To really enjoy the *amour*," urged one of the most idolized of Hollywood's male film stars, "it must be a matter of life and death."[20]

This ideal, serious as it was, ultimately remained innocent and superficial. The very style of romance functioned as a protection against dangerous intimacy. Even the rituals of courtship served to inhibit deep emotional growth between a young man and woman. The Lynds noted a "growing tendency to engage in leisure-time pursuits by couples rather than in crowds, the unattached man or woman being more 'out of it' in the highly paired social life of [the twenties] than a generation ago when informal 'dropping in' was the rule." While this type of "dating" encouraged early coupling, personal intimacy and sexual exploration were still considered taboo.[21]

New public institutions catered to this trend. Although urban amusements did provide an atmosphere for moral experimentation and mingling of the sexes that would have been scandalous in the nineteenth century, the environment was still highly controlled. The cabaret, for example, had been elevated from a vice to a legitimate public amusement in the early 1900s. In cabarets, couples could experience erotic excitement: dancing, stimulating music, and a romantic aura. Certainly there was more physical contact in the cabaret than genteel culture would have permitted in previous generations. But the setting essentially precluded any real intimacy. Loud music thwarted any serious conversation; the show provided structure, and all were encouraged to participate. F. Scott Fitzgerald claimed that the era of the flapper "brought the nice girl into the cabaret and sat her down next to the distinctly non-nice girl." The significance was that she could still remain the nice girl.[22]

Even dancing, while physically close, remained innocent. One observer of the dance craze perceived, "As only the young danced, the activity was seen as a childish endeavor, to be relinquished shortly after marriage."[23] Since it was something young couples did during courtship, it was supposed to provide good, clean fun and healthy recreation—devoid of sensuality. Irene and Vernon Castle did the most to uplift cabaret dancing into middle-class respectability, and they bacame major public figures during the teens. Irene Castle was one of the first "flappers" to bob her hair; she was youthful, active, and healthy. It was the Castles who took the potentially seductive dance and made it "fun." "If Vernon had ever looked into my eyes with smoldering passion during the tango," Irene explained, "we should have both burst out laughing." Thus dancing became a means to experience physical closeness and erotic excitement, without the dangers of sexuality.[24]

As with dancing, the motion picture was another potentially dangerous activity legitimized during the Progressive era. Eroticism and sensuality on the screen offered a vicarious thrill, but virtue always triumphed in the end. Heroes and heroines proved themselves worthy of true love. Invariably, the happy ending focused on wedded bliss. Young people watching these cinematic moral lessons learned the styles of romance. But the message of the plot reinforced the need for restraint. Love-struck viewers might hold hands or embrace in the darkened theaters; but not much else could happen. They sat in a public place, facing the screen without talking to each other, watching attractive film idols instruct them in the art of gaining allure without losing virtue. While the happy ending remained idealized matrimony, a traditional American theme, there was an important shift in emphasis. The same ends were now reached by new means: flirtation, beauty, youthful activity, and consumer spending.[25]

The rituals of courtship, then, were largely superficial. In keeping with the stress on personality and attraction, total openness and honesty were often discouraged, even after the marriage had taken place. One of Muncie's leading ministers in the twenties asserted, "One thing I always tell my young men

when they marry, is that they must get over any habit of
thinking that they must be frank and tell everything they know
to their wives." Dorothy Dix agreed, advocating illusions
rather than reality:

"Let well enough alone" is a fine matrimonial slogan and as
long as husband and wife are good actors it is the part of
wisdom for their mates not to pry too deeply into the motives
that inspire their conduct. . . . What we don't know doesn't
hurt us in domestic life, and the wise do not try to find out too
much. . . . Nothing does more to *preserve the illusions* that a
man and woman have about each other than the things they
don't know.[26]

The formula, then, was to hide one's true nature, and keep
each other busy having fun. It was a matter of perfecting a
technique, rather than deepening an intimate relationship. We
find this style emanating most effusively from Hollywood, the
center of the romantic lifestyle and, significantly, within the
locale of our study. Film stars, often outspoken on the matter
of love, advocated the code in their public statements as well
as on screen. And it was not just women, but men, too, who
were expected to cultivate romance. Wallace Reid advised
male readers "to begin the A-B-C's of how to keep friend wife
happy enough at home so she won't insist on more than one
evening out a week." The idea was to make matrimony a continual game. "If a man can learn to play golf, he can learn to
play marriage."[27]

In keeping with this outer-directedness, Judge Bartlett of the
Reno Divorce Court warned,

The bride should be very sure that she has reflected on what
other people think and feel about her young man. . . . After the
first flush of marriage happiness the bride is going to judge her
man by much the same standards as others judge him. If he
hasn't measured up before to public opinion, the chances are
strongly against his measuring up to her private opinion in the
second year after the great event.[28]

Wives were instructed in the art of "keeping" as well as
"catching" a husband. A writer in *Photoplay*, describing the
Hollywood style, offered this bit of advice: "Women are matrimonial ostriches. They hide their heads in the sands of virtue
and moral law and refuse to admit that marriage is a competi-

tive game in which *getting* a husband is merely the first trick."[29] External qualities were stressed at the expense of more serious concerns. As one recent study points out:

Personal attractiveness and appearance of the girl and attractiveness of the young man as well as his rating as a "good spender" often take precedence in young minds over practical considerations of stability and the ability to shoulder the responsibilities of marriage and children.[30]

What, then, were the immediate effects of the cult of youth and romance on personal relationships? What was the impact of new urban amusements and economic abundance? Potentially, the results could be positive. Women as well as men had the opportunity to ease out of Victorian strictures and lead more expressive, experiential, and even playful lives. But without integration into a totally new way of life, including changed attitudes, moral codes, and a revised and realistic concept of marriage, these new elements could foster frustrations. For despite new possibilities for unique relationships, couples were encouraged to conform to a popular ideal of flirtation, urged to become obsessive about appearance and youth, and warned against too much intimacy or even honesty. At the same time, romance was to guarantee ultimate happiness. For women, finding and catching the right man was the key to personal fulfillment—the very essence of life. As a consequence of the elevated hopes surrounding love and marriage, husbands who did not provide the proper magic for their wives might be discarded in the divorce court. For men, attractive, exciting young women were appealing. But this allure could not sustain a marriage. For both sexes, the romantic style distorted expectations for marriage. It served as no real preparation for a deep mutual relationship of openness and intimacy.

"Let us be honest," wrote Lavinia Hart, "we expected 'perfect happiness.'" She was aware of the dangers of romantic illusions, for "the way of young lovers is to hide their true selves and pretend to be something a great deal better, and for this they pay dearly."[31] Hart did not realize that the mode of love she advocated for her *Cosmopolitan* readers led directly into this path. Nevertheless, it was an ideal geared to perfecting marriage. According to the formulas expounded in popular culture, a romantic courtship would lead to a modern marriage.

The couple, presumably, would establish a family in a tranquil suburban neighborhood, where the restlessness generated by twentieth-century life could be safely contained and indulged. Like the residents of Los Angeles, urbanites all over the country hoped that an expanded and perfected home—complete with youthful adults, exciting leisure activities, and an abundance of consumer goods—might compensate for frustrating or alienating public and economic endeavors. However, given the enormous expectations for personal fulfillment focused on home and family life, marriage might turn out to be disappointing. Indeed, in the early decades of the twentieth century, dissatisfied spouses increasingly turned toward the divorce courts.

II

Matrimony Unveiled in the Early Twentieth Century

Five

The Romantic Ideal in Crisis

The formula for modern marriage and family life radiated from Los Angeles to the entire nation. Americans looked toward this western city and saw what appeared to be a warm suburban paradise filled with happy and prosperous men and women, living romantic, affluent lives. Movies certainly gave this vision immediacy and power, but it was not merely a cinematic fantasy. The idealized home seen on the screen became a reality in Hollywood, where movie stars lived the good life. A symbol even more than a place, Hollywood came to represent suburban home life par excellence. For the stars gave the appearance of being ordinary folks and served as models for popular identification and emulation. Perhaps even more than their media images, the widely publicized "private" lives of motion picture celebrities had profound impact across the nation.

What followed after the happy ending? In Los Angeles, the happy endings seemed to come off the screen into real life. The Hollywood style deserves careful scrutiny, for it represents the pinnacle of the modern marriage ideal. It was the habitat of film idols whose off-screen lives epitomized the fulfillment of modern expectations for personal happiness. While Hollywood became most noted as the film capital of the world, perhaps of equal importance during these years was its clear identification with an entirely new type of home.[1]

One of the most dramatic expressions of this modern domestic ideal emerged with the union of two of Hollywood's most adored screen stars of the teens, Douglas Fairbanks and Mary Pickford. In 1920, they each obtained a divorce in order to marry the other. The stigma of scandal from the suggestion of adultery leading to the divorces quickly wore off, and the new union was declared the "most successful and famous marriage the world has ever known." Throughout the twenties, "Doug and Mary" were the focus of much attention; dozens of articles described their home and lifestyle. Typical was one by a Hollywood writer who proclaimed the duo's union as an "amazing marriage" at a time when others fail. The key to their marital success lay in elevating the home above all other concerns in life, and excluding all sordid elements from its walls. "Pickfair"—their elaborate Hollywood estate—was "the crown of their happiness." Materially, it was a consumer's paradise, complete with all the accompaniments to leisure living from tennis courts to an army of servants. But it was more than luxury that made Pickfair the focus of mass envy; it was the creation of a totally self-contained private universe.

To maintain their idyllic domestic haven, the Fairbankses left all the cares of the studio behind them, and built a "bulwark" against the world. The writer called them "the two most home-loving people I have ever known." In accord with the ideals of the youth cult, Mary was known as "America's Sweetheart," the epitome of childlike innocence; and Doug was the flamboyant and athletic "eternal youth." They combined their youthfulness and high-level affluence into Pickfair, the "center of life." Not only did they physically isolate their private domain, but they refused to let concerns of the world penetrate its walls. "Nothing comes before their home." Sparing each other worries and sorrow, their time together was not a "dumping ground" for the concerns of the day. They put no "unnecessary burdens" on their married life.[2] Ironically, however, this idealized marriage ended in divorce, and Doug and Mary each went on to a third spouse. Nevertheless, the union of Fairbanks and Pickford deserves careful consideration. For if their marriage symbolized anything, it was the ultimate realization—and subsequent failure—of the self-contained privatized home geared to personal happiness.

The marriage of the famous Hollywood couple was clearly an extension of the youth cult: fun, carefree, innocent, and consciously devoid of the serious concerns of life. According to the formula, youthfulness was an essential element for marriage. As we have seen, the marriage age dropped steadily during the decades under consideration, for men as well as women (see table 10). Although economic prosperity no doubt encouraged early matrimony, the attempt to capture youth within wedlock may have also contributed to this trend.

Youth, however, does not last forever; and as Americans married younger, they divorced more often. A number of studies have shown that young marriages are more susceptible to divorce. We can see this reflected in the data. Although the divorce samples include second marriages, we still see a downward trend over time. In the 1920 Los Angeles sample, where it is possible to control for first or second unions, the marriage age is lower than the national average. Undoubtedly, this is a complex phenomenon involving many causal factors, but the statistics suggest that day-to-day married life did not meet the promises of the Hollywood style. It is not likely that many people accepted the ideal of youth and romance as a total way of life; but apparently it did influence expectations surrounding marriage. If the man desired a young wife, all the cosmetics, clothes, and styles that "money could buy" would not prevent the aging process. In the 1920 divorce samples, we find that this did indeed create tensions.

Conflicts involving personal appearance and youthfulness were not found in the 1880s proceedings. They do appear, however, in the 1920 cases. One New Jersey man apparently left his wife because her looks "annoyed" him. After seven years of marriage, which included six moves and one child, Harold Van Piper deserted his wife Bertha. When he left, he told her bluntly, "Bert, I am simply tired of you and furthermore you are getting too fat, you are too much of the washerwoman type for me." When she implored him to stay on behalf of their child, he replied, "Are you not big enough and fat enough to make your own living?" If Bertha did become overweight, it is not surprising. She complained that Harold rarely took her anywhere; "oftentimes, I was not out of the house for weeks at a time, I simply took care of the baby." Bertha was granted the divorce.[3]

In 1920 Los Angeles, the center of the youth and beauty cult, these issues appeared more often in the divorce cases. We find twelve men indicating dissatisfaction with their spouses' looks, or with the inevitable process of aging. One was James Whitman. He married Adella in a small Kansas town, they lived together seventeen years, and had no children. Adella Whitman considered herself a "person of refined and cultured

tastes and sensibilities, having been a school teacher a number
of years." But these qualities, it seemed, were not enough to
satisfy her husband. In her complaints of cruelty, she claimed
that James had not only called her a fool, but had taunted,
"I'm going to get myself a woman, then I'll be ready for the
day's work. And you can get yourself a man. I think that will
be all right, don't you?" He also told her, "You are too old.
I'm getting myself a young woman." Adella felt that her husband's actions "rendered impossible the sacred objects, aims,
and purposes of the divine institution of marriage." These
charges suggest that James and Adella, after seventeen years
together, had come to hold different ideas as to what marriage
ought to be. To the husband, it was for youthful regeneration
and excitement. To the wife, it was sacred and pure.[4]

A similar case was that of Charles and Edna Widam, both
clerks, who had married in Batavia, Ohio, in 1900, and had two
children. Among her complaints of cruelty, Edna claimed that
her husband "tells her she is getting old and he likes to be with
young girls." But this was not the only difficulty troubling this
wife. Owing to Charles' neglect to provide, Edna had been
compelled to work for the previous two years to provide for
herself and her children, although Charles earned good wages.
She also charged him with being "violent when drunk...a
disgusting sight and...often abusive." Moreover, after she
had worked for the grocery money, he complained about her
cooking. This husband was somewhat ambivalent about what
he wanted from his marriage partner. Although he was enam-
ored with youth, and enjoyed young girls, he also wanted a
mate who was a good wife and homemaker. Yet he was less
fastidious about his own obligations, for in their thirteen years
together, they moved nine times, six for failure to pay the rent.
The court granted the divorce to Edna, plus custody of the
children and $40 per month. Charles Widam could not sustain a
marriage with his conflicting ideals of women. He grew to neglect and disdain his wife, because she could not remain eter-
nally young and hold a job, as well as cultivate the arts of
cooking and homemaking all at once.[5]

According to the divorces filed in Los Angeles in 1920, ordinary couples did not find it easy to live according to the formulas expounded by their famous Hollywood neighbors. Husbands like James Whitman and Charles Widam were torn by
desires for both excitement and purity; and few women could

satisfy both. Some men were attracted to the sensual "new woman," but then wanted virtuous wives. John Kuntz, for example, married an attractive young girl and proceeded to try to knock virtue into her. Gladys Kuntz complained to the court of her husband's tyrannical cruelty, claiming that he never supported her, forbade her even to speak with former boyfriends; and "made her put on long dresses; said he hadn't married the cradle." At one point, after he had kicked her, the girl's brother admonished him. Curiously, the brother objected to the husband's means, not his ultimate ends. Saying that he was "a man old enough to have sense and that Gladys was only a child," he urged his brother-in-law to "overlook her faults . . . train her instead of abusing her. . . . He always said he would tame her, that he would break her." After living with John one year, Gladys obtained a divorce and the return of her maiden name.[6]

Similarly, Jane and Fred Tilmann were married in 1918, he a thirty-three-year-old pattern maker from Germany, and she a thirty-eight-year-old widowed movie actress from Texas. Although Fred may have been initially attracted by his wife's glamorous life, he changed his attitude toward her once they were married. He admonished her, tore up all her clothes, and threw them on the floor. He made her "dress to his taste, and . . . would refuse to permit her to wear gloves, or silk hosiery while shopping in the downtown business district of the city." He told his wife's married daughter that he only married her through pity, and that she was woman of bad character. He also accused her of cooking "slop," and said that he would "go back to Germany to marry a woman who could be a wife and who did not have dirty American ways." Undoubtedly, it was the actress's "dirty American ways." that attracted him in the first place. But once the marriage had taken place, he—like John Kuntz—wanted to remove those sensual elements from the home. Jane Tilmann was granted the divorce by default.[7]

While these men married exciting women and then wanted moral spouses, others married for purity but later wanted something more. Several husbands who lost interest in their wives felt both guilty and inadequate because they could not be worthy of the true women they had wed. Some actually defended their wives as pinnacles of respectability, even though they no longer wished to be married to them. One such case was that of Margaret and James Wingham, who had married when he was a fifty-nine-year-old widower and she a fifty-seven-year-old spinster. Margaret Wingham filed the suit, claiming that James, superintendent at an oil refinery, deserted her after only six months of living together. James wrote a letter to his wife's brother indicating that he felt unworthy of her. He claimed that the split was "caused entirely by my inability to measure up to her standards of what a husband should be... I confess it, regretfully and in humiliation... we are simply too old to adjust our different natures to meet on a common plane.... There is no blame whatever to be attached to her.... We shall remain friends and she shall want for nothing material for her comfort. It has been a hideous mistake—she has taken the only sane and honorable way to end it." James also wrote to his wife:

I believe that no better woman lives, and I am willing to concede that your life is on a higher plane than my own.... I am not worthy and cannot appreciate the wealth of affection you appear to have thrown away on me... the dream is over—good bye Maggie but permit me to remain your sincere, faithful friend—Jim.

The ironic tragedy in this case was that Margaret Wingham had no such dismal thoughts concerning their union, and apparently wished to continue the marriage. Although James considered her life "on a higher plane" than his own, he was the one eager for divorce. It appears as though James thought he wanted a wife to uplift him, but it only took him six months to realize that he actually preferred the "lower plane" of his former life. A second, more forceful letter from James to Margaret intimated this conflict: "I have tried by every means in my power to tell you and make you understand in a kindly and considerate way that our relations as man and wife are at an end, but you seem to ignore it altogether."[8]

Despite his obvious boredom with her virtue, James Wingham upheld his wife as a model of true womanhood. He was similar to several other ambivalent Los Angeles husbands in the 1920 sample who considered themselves morally inferior the their wives. Another was Thomas Foster, whose wife Gertrude had sued him for divorce on the grounds of cruelty. She claimed that he had constantly nagged, quarreled with and cursed her when she was in "extremely delicate condition of health and of a highly nervous and sensitive disposition." Her husband answered by accusing her of extravagance, wastefulness, and having a "proud and overbearing and tyrannical disposition." He claimed that "he at all times used all reasonable endeavors to induce her not to desert and abandon him and stay at home and to do her housework and keep house and demean herself as a housewife," but she persisted in "picking up and following avocations, such as hairdresser, nurse, electrician, telegraph operator, and any business or calling that would take her away from her home duties and the society and company of her husband." Although Gertrude sounded like something of a Renaissance woman, her husband preferred a one-dimensional housewife to a female jack-of-all trades. Gertrude was granted the divorce.

Later, on reflection, Thomas Foster had second thoughts and realized that, despite her outrageous conduct and reckless spending, he still believed that she was a pure and virtuous woman. "I must have been hard to live with," he confessed. "I am learning my lesson now. I can't eat or sleep. Do not hate me, Gertie, for I love you and always will love you." Finally he restored his wife to the exalted position of moral female on a pedestal:

I will do anything you want me to do. The things you wanted me to do I now see would not hurt me. Your were *uplifting* and not lowering me. I now see . . . I do not want to see you working, Gertie, while I am able to work. I love you . . . I will be nice to you and never speak cross to you. I will always raise my hat to you and I will always help you.[9]

In all these cases, regardless of specific complaints, the consistent theme was the desire for the new vitality and the old morality to coexist within the home. But judging from these conflicts, the domestic realm could not easily sustain both at once.

The tension often came to focus in the area of night life and amusements, which by 1920 had become a common source of marital discord. In the 1880s, it was usually men who were accused of overindulgence in amusements and "vice." Even wives who behaved improperly rarely frequented entertainment zones. In the later period, however, this pattern had changed markedly. With the proliferation and legitimization of amusements catering to both sexes, women were drawn increasingly to urban night life. As we have seen, leisure activities such as movies and cabarets had become an accepted part of courtship. But if a wife remained attracted to these places after marriage—especially if her husband wanted her to "settle down"—friction might result. Indeed, in the 1920 Los Angeles sample, although wives still accused their husbands of drinking and gambling, twice as many men as women complained about their spouses' involvement in night life and amusements (see table 9).

Certainly, men frequented dance halls, cabarets, and other types of entertainments as much as women, if not more. Traditionally, these had been places where a man was expected to "let off steam." Unless such endeavors became "habits," or seriously impaired his ability to function as a proper husband, they were tolerated. But "respectable" women took no part in these activities until the turn of the century. Although cabarets and movie houses were becoming legitimate amusements for middle-class women in the early decades of the twentieth century, not all men condoned their wives' indulgence.

Edna Newton was one such woman whose participation in nightlife annoyed her husband. She came to Los Angeles from Colorado in 1916 and married Fred Newton, an accountant. They had two children. According to Fred, Edna had an "insatiable desire to attend cabarets where she would insist upon remaining nearly all night, aginst the wishes of her husband, who repeatedly tried to induce her to care for their children." But she claimed that if he refused to go with her, she would go alone, and she continually begged him "once more to go to Venice and have one more good time."[10]

John Bayer was another husband who asserted that his spouse was only concerned with having fun. A witness on his behalf testified that his wife "never had any love for him . . . she never made a home, she was no home maker, she would rather be out on the street than in her home any time."[11] In a similar case, Edward Moley filed for divorce from his wife Faye, claiming that "no damn man living could keep her from going to dances or doing as she pleased and it was none of his business what she did, and that she expected to continue to dance and go to dances as long as she liked."[12] Another such freedom-loving woman was Fay Dial, who had been married only three weeks when she went to a dance alone and returned at 1:30 A. M. When her husband complained, she picked up her suitcase and left, saying that married life was too slow, and she did not propose to be confined in such a way.[13]

If some men disliked their wives' participation in night life, some women found their mates' lack of enthusiasm frustrating. One former flapper, recalling her younger years, expressed a fervent desire for excitement that was not shared by her spouse. Married to her fourth husband, and comfortably retired from various occupations ranging from Hollywood hairdresser to teacher on an Indian reservation, she explained why she divorced her first husband in Idaho and came to Los Angeles in the early twenties: "He never wanted to go anywhere or do anything. He was a jerk, dear."[14]

Some women whose husbands were reluctant to go out with them found other men more amenable. Willie Miller, for example, married John Miller in Mississippi, in 1896. After six children and twenty-three years of marriage, Willie apparently wanted something more out of life. According to her husband, their problems began when she took an office job in 1917, and soon began going out every night until late. Her husband, a salesman who was often away on business, found that she was spending a great deal of time with her employer, Sam Gaynor. Not only did she refuse to quit her job, but he discovered that she often went to theaters, restaurants, and cafes in the amusement centers of Venice and Vernon, and was seen dining and dancing with Gaynor. Although Willie denied any improper conduct, John was granted the divorce; and Willie went on to marry Gaynor.[15]

The marriage of George and Marguerite Fawcett had a similar fate. The couple married in 1915, when he was a twenty-six-year-old carpenter, and she a twenty-two-year-old Iowan. After three years of marriage and one child, they separated. George claimed that Marguerite would go out often when he was in the service, and continued to do so after he returned. She went out drinking at cafes and other "questionable resorts," leaving him with their baby. Once she returned at one o'clock in the morning "with her clothes disarranged and undone, smelling of liquor." Finally he accused her of adultry "in a taxi-cab on West Jefferson Street," and he left her that day.

George requested custody of the child, claiming that his wife
was unfit.[16]

These proceedings suggest that women may have been more
attracted to the new urban amusements than men. It is also
possible that the men simply complained about it more.
Perhaps wives were more inclined to expect and tolerate their
husbands' indulgence in these activities. Even in 1920, when
public entertainments had opened up to both sexes, it remained difficult for men to accept their wives' proclivities for
"forbidden" excitement. The legal system reinforced these
feelings. In most cases, judges were sympathetic with husbands who complained of their wives' inclinations. There were
some, however, who recognized these desires and considered
them legitimate. One judge put it this way:

Excitement to most women is a drug that either stimulates or
soothes. To many women it is necessary. To all healthy
women it is a sought-after part of their existence.... Where a
man sublimates much of his nervous energy in the struggle to
make a living, a woman must have recourse to activities that
seem silly to him.[17]

Without quite realizing it, this judge made a fierce stab at the
conditions of modern life that forced men to "sublimate"
through work, and created bored women who felt the need for
"silly" stimulation. More and more women were participating
in leisure endeavors, often at the expense of what many husbands felt were their domestic responsibilities. We have seen
how this disrupted several marriages in Los Angeles in 1920. In
New Jersey at the same time, we find even more illuminating
cases of this nature. Since the divorces were filed on a
statewide basis, they include urban as well as rural residents.
Tensions between the farm and the city stand out in bold relief
in this largely rural, yet also highly industrialized, state.

The New Jersey cases are filled with conflicts surrounding
women's participation in urban life. It is interesting to note that
not one case in the 225 examined included the reverse complaint: men being drawn to amusement arenas. Conflicts
emerged when wives burst out of former restraints and dove
head first into new and unexplored territory. Typical was the
case of Edith Zerbe, who "wanted to live in a large city, saying
the county was too slow for her." Twenty-year-old Edith, who

worked in a shoe factory, had married Harry, a chocolate maker working in Hershey, Pennsylvania, in 1908. Two years later she deserted. Although Harry said he "worked hard and did everything in my power to please her and provide a comfortable and suitable home for her," she apparently grew tired of the small-town life they led. "We never had any serious quarrels... my wife never wanted for anything within my means to get for her, but no matter how hard I tried to please her and get along, she quarreled all the time and said she was dissatisfied with married life and wanted to be free again." His mother concurred, saying, "She never made any charge about my son's conduct toward her. At times she would use violent language about the town and the people, cursing them in general." The court granted Harry the divorce.[18]

In a similar case, Maude Grossman, also a laborer, left her clerk and farmer husband in 1917, after three years of marriage. They were wed when she was twenty and he nineteen, and had one child. The couple lived on Andrew's parents' farm, and according to the state interviewer, Maude was "tired of living on a farm." Andrew explained, "My wife frequently complained that she was dissatisfied to live where we were living, and I mean by this our farm. She was fond of moving pictures and wanted to go [to her home town] most of her time, where things were more active." Backing up his son and their rural way of life, Andrew's father articulated the essence of traditional virtue:

Andrew has lived on our farm since his wife deserted him. Andrew is a boy of good habits. He never uses liquor or tobacco. He is a church member and a good boy. He has always been industrious and works every day. He has always been a good worker. My farm is plentifully stocked and it could not be possible for anyone to live on my farm and not have plenty to eat."

Maude never defended herself, and Andrew won his suit.[19]

Others with inclinations similar to those of Maude Grossman included Mary Ford, who found the town of Green Back "too dead... not lively enough," or May Stone, who was "fond of fast living," or Elizabeth Fowler, who enjoyed "the gay life" and deserted her husband to go to Atlantic City. Gabriella Clark "craved excitement and change... life in Trenton wasn't fast enough for her and she wanted to have a good time." Marian Gross liked the "sporty life . . . if she wanted to go to the theater, she would go in spite of everything. She would go and leave my little girl alone—I went to work at about seven in the morning, and the folks there told me that I would not be gone fifteen minutes before she would go out." All of these wives were married to blue-collar husbands; they all deserted, and their husbands were granted divorces.[20]

It is interesting to note that these wives did not defend themselves or make excuses for their conduct, as did the 1880s wives who tried to argue that their activities all fell within the line of duty. In the later samples, some women readily admitted their lack of interest in traditional roles. Sarah Haydrick, for example, was a young New Jersey wife who knew nothing about housekeeping, and cared even less. According to her mother-in-law, "During the time they were living with me, I discovered the wife knew little or nothing about cooking and I tried to teach her, telling her that she ought to learn so she could do it when she kept house for her husband. She said she didn't want to keep house—that if she had thought of it when she got married . . . she would not have gotten married." After a year of wedlock, she deserted. When Andrew saw her the following year, she told him she was happy, under no obligation to anyone and wanted to stay that way. Andrew Haydrick won his suit for divorce.[21]

One husband was acutely aware of the lure of city life and the effect it had on his wife. In this case it was the wife who filed for divorce. Emma Neal claimed that her husband Clarence was violent and cruel toward her. In their two-year marriage, they moved often, and she worked as a bookkeeper. Neighbors testified that Clarence beat his wife; but his blows apparently did not have their desired effect, and he tried something new. Before moving to Evesboro, Clarence declared that he was "going to take her down in the country where he could fix her feet for her, that he couldn't tame her down in the city but would tame her down there all right." Emma won her suit.[22]

In another intriguing case, it was not merely the wife's indulgence that infuriated her husband, but the fact that she insisted upon flying solo. Thomas Nestor complained bitterly that his wife neglected her household duties in favor of urban attractions. "I do everything for the boys," he said, "I do their washing and ironing for them and look after their clothes. I did and still do." He was a factory machinest who worked nights, and he said that he knew his wife Nora, a thread worker, "flirted around" because the sheets never looked used in the morning. This Catholic couple lived together twelve years and had two sons. Finally in exasperation Thomas told her that she would "have to cut out running around nights and would have to do her duty as a wife, and I said if she wanted to go to a theater, moving picture or a dance, I thought it was about time for her, the children and I to go together; that I had been tied down in the house like a dog taking care of the children all the time when she was out. So she said, 'If that is the case, I am going to get the dickens out and go where I feel like it.'" Thomas was awarded the divorce, plus custody of the children.[23]

There are several important aspects of these cases worth noting, especially when comparing them to the divorces of the 1880s. For one thing, these wives were berated for their neglect of duties or for their seemingly unreasonable demands upon their husbands, many of whom could not afford the time, energy or money to supply the "good times" their restless wives craved. But while these types of complaints increased numerically in the later years, they carried fewer harsh character references about the women. These wives may have been frivolous, selfish, or irresponsible, but—unless they were carousing with other men—their chastity was not an issue. Clearly, amusements for women were becoming more acceptable. Moreover, if men and women enjoyed these pursuits together, all the better. It was believed that couples who "played together" might have happier marriages and healthier lives— which may well have been true. But if the married partners were not able to integrate these desires into a compatible relationship, trouble might ensue. As a result, the union could end with the accusation that the woman was a bad *wife*, but not necessarily a totally evil, depraved or disreputable "whore." This appears all the more intriguing when viewed in light of the 1880s cases, where the very moral fiber of a frivolous woman was often maligned.

By 1920, then, a moderate amount of leisure and amusement was considered good healthy fun for both sexes, provided it did not interfere with domestic responsibilities, and as long as both spouses shared the inclination equally. This shift was part of an altered conception of home life, and, accordingly, changing ideas about matrimony. Gradually the notion of personal happiness began to loom larger and larger as a component of marriage. But this new emphasis was not without its problems. With so much concern placed upon the happiness of the married partners, what about children? The image of marriage in the popular culture left little room for parental responsibilities. It is no accident that Douglas Fairbanks and Mary Pickford had no children, that the couples in the Hollywood movies were also childless, and that the entire issue of offspring was conspicuously lacking in the advice columns on matrimonial bliss. Yet among the population at large, children were indeed a very real part of marriage and home life. Predictably, some of the most bitter conflicts to appear in the divorce cases revolved around the children.

In spite of the increasing stress on romance and youth, active young brides were still expected to accept motherhood with total delight and absorption. The problem was that an all-or-nothing decision about having a family faced every woman at marriage. If she chose children, she would probably have to deny any desires for a career or active public life. If she resisted motherhood, she was subject to social stigma and condemnation. If she desired both, she would almost certainly have difficulties. Jobs rarely allowed for a mother's scheduling needs, and husbands were often either unwilling or unable to share childrearing responsibilities. Unless a woman was affluent enough as well as willing to turn her child over to the care of a servant, she had virtually no recourse but to give up many opportunities open to her. Children remained the responsibility of mothers.

Whatever new options for work or leisure were available to women, the complicating factor was inevitably children. If they had them, what would they do with them. If they chose not to, it meant facing fierce criticism and social ostracism. Women with no desire for children were considered not only irresponsible but unnatural. Females were assumed to be maternal by nature. "Love of offspring is in man a cultivated emotion; in women an instinct," wrote one "expert." "There are women lacking the instinct as there are calves born with

two heads, but for the purpose of generalization these exceptions may be ignored."[24] Accordingly, in cases of divorce,
even if the husband filed suit, custody of the children almost
always went to the wife (see table 11).

By 1920, the average American family had fewer children
than in the previous century. Yet childlessness was not advocated. Even the neo-Malthusians and birth control advocates
urged families to limit their children, but not to renege totally
on their procreative duty. Offspring were expected to result
from marriage, and they automatically fell to the care of
women. In all the samples, very few wives admitted having no
desire for children. One case in Los Angeles in 1920 is important because of its very uniqueness. Albert Stanford claimed
that his wife refused to live with him, "giving as a reason... that the marriage relation is not congenial to her and
that she desired to pursue the intellectual life. That she has no
particular affection for her child and does not have the maternal instinct." Substantiating his claim was a letter from his
wife, Vance:

Your letter dated February 23 received. ...I definitely and
positively refuse to link up my life again with yours. ... If as
you say you are compelled to seek a divorce from me, I am
quite willing that you should have the legal custody of our
child, provided as you say in your letter, that I have legal
access to her at all times and am considered in the welfare of
her future. Yours in friendship, Vance.

What is more remarkable than the tone of this letter is that, in
the era of the rise of the independent woman, this was the
only case of its kind in any of the samples.[25]

Rather than rejecting motherhood in favor of other pursuits,
women were more likely to place hopes for happiness in their
children. Accordingly, childrearing took on new meaning in
order to fit into the "fun morality" of the leisure lifestyle. The
strict discipline of the nineteenth century geared to raising pure
and moral individuals gave way to indulgence as mothers focused their own need for amusement on their children. With
little else offering sustained personal involvement, women
turned with intensified commitment to home and family.

In the matter of motherhood, most women in the divorce
samples expressed traditional domestic inclinations. Although

the presence of offspring may have inhibited inclinations for divorce, slightly over half of the couples in all the samples had children (see table 12). Not surprisingly, more men than women were accused of abusive conduct toward children (see table 13). Yet for a woman to reject her maternal responsibilities was one of the most heinous offenses a wife could commit. Those who did not wish to have children at all were considered virtually criminal. Esther Sachs, for example, a Los Angeles wife in 1920, "wrongfully and improperly refused and still refuses to become pregnant or to remain pregnant," and "insisted upon committing abortions."[26] This was sufficient cause for divorce, if it was against the husband's will. As we see in table 13, however, this was relatively rare. Only four Los Angeles men in 1920 complained that their wives did not want children; and none made such an accusation in the 1880s. Rather than rejecting youngsters, women tended to center the family life upon them.[27]

It would be misleading to assume, however, that these attitudes were imposed upon women by their husbands or the outside society. Indeed, women were among the most forceful advocates of the maternal ideal. One wife, for example, considered her childrearing duties not merely a chore, but a right. Bertha Nields charged her husband Harry with cruelty, after twenty years of marriage and seven children. She claimed that he wanted her to "go out and work and leave the children to care for themselves." Bertha requested separate maintenance, custody of the children, and a restraining order preventing her husband from visiting them. But shortly thereafter she reconsidered and wrote to her lawyer asking him to dismiss the case. "We have become reconciled," she explained, "and for the children's sake will start a new home and life over again."[28]

By 1920, we find that the ideal of marriage had evolved somewhat ambiguously. Matrimony was intended to promote the happiness of the spouses. A certain amount of fun and amusement was expected as part of the bargain. At the same time, children were anticipated and the familial responsibilities of both husbands and wives remained virtually unchallenged. Women wanted their mates to be good providers as well as fun-loving pals; men desired wives who were exciting as well as virtuous. On the whole, couples hoped that marriage would include fewer sacrifices and more satisfactions. But obviously, the Hollywood formula was not the answer. Although it did represent a genuine cultural ideal, couples could not do away with the serious responsibilities of married life and children, even if they so desired. There were, indeed, new aspirations for fun and excitement, but these alone could not sustain a marriage. What, then, were the alternatives? Modern styles and amusements comprised only part of the enormous transformation taking place in America. The emerging urban culture had many other components, among them the "sexual revolution," the influx of women into the work force, and the rise of consumer spending. All presented new options for both men and women, and had a profound impact on domestic life. But as we shall see, the transition into modern life was neither smooth nor complete. When combined with persistent Victorian holdovers, new expectations could lead to new tensions.

Six
Sex: Sin or Salvation

As twentieth-century Americans turned away from the ascetic codes of the past, they began to shed the Victorian reticence concerning sex. By 1920 the desirability of sexual delights within marriage had captured the public imagination. Liberal thinkers expounded upon the issue, vehemently arguing that sexual repression was unhealthy. Marriage should allow the full flowering of physical pleasure, for both men and women. During the second decade of the century lovemaking texts became popular reading. One promised

Sixty-four pages of male/female positional photographs ... intercourse innovations and sexual variants which best satisfy a seeking mate's *orgasmic need*.... It transforms same-old-thing "bedroom encounters" into excitingly different LOVE AFFAIRS—again, again and again ... passionately banishes the sameness of old-hat sex. Can any marriage, anchored to this solid *bed*rock of unsuppressed voluptuous sexual variety fail to become stronger?

Perhaps here was the answer to modern restlessness: marriage could provide ultimate personal fulfillment through sexual gratification. But this was easier said than done, for Victorian attitudes in this delicate matter were not easily shed. The problem was complicated by the fact that it was only sex between wedded spouses that gained sanction—not erotic indulgence outside the bonds of matrimony. For despite new roles, amusements, leisure, and an emphasis on self-expression, one of the most persistent social values to remain intact from the nineteenth to the twentieth century was the taboo against premarital sex.[1]

During the Victorian era, this maxim fit well into a general ascetic attitude toward life, extending into work and leisure as well as sexual relations—both prior to and during marriage. Nineteenth-century writers on the subject generally considered it both immoral and dangerous if conjugal relations took place more than once or twice a month. In 1870, Henry James expressed this Victorian idea by stating that the purpose of marriage "is to educate us out of our animal beginnings."[2] Self-control was bred into children from their early years, as a protection against the temptations of the flesh that would emerge as they neared physical maturity. One nineteenth-century advisor of male youth warned of the dangers to both the individual and society:

If a young man only follow the impulses of his appetites and passions, he will retard the general return to true order, and secure for himself that unhappiness in the future which is the invariable consequence.[3]

In the 1830s, Tocqueville perceived that Americans made concerted efforts in order to repress their sexual instincts. If asceticism was necessary for men in order to compete effectively in the laissez-faire economy, it was equally important for women, for purity was essential in the open marriage market. Chastity, in the fluid and mobile society of nineteenth-century towns and cities, marked the difference between "good" and "bad" women. The competitive spirit of democracy placed great emphasis on individual virtues as determinants of success or failure. For both sexes, personal asceticism was a prerequisite for achievement in their most important pursuits: work for men and marriage for women. But purity was not to be attained through external repression or protection. Rather, in accordance with the ideals of the liberal state, it was to be built into the individual will. For women, whose lives were geared toward marriage and family, there were fewer active outlets for energy than were available to men. Self-discipline, therefore, had to be carefully taught. As Tocqueville perceived,

Believing that they had little chance of repressing in woman the most vehement passions of the human heart, they held that the surer way was to teach her the art of combatting those passions for herself. . . . They made vigorous efforts to cause individual independence to control itself to defend the virtue of women.[4]

This moral code appears to have been effective. Using the proportion of brides who were pregnant at marriage as an index of premarital sexual activity, Daniel Scott Smith found a steady decline from 1800 to the 1870s, when the trend began to shift.[5]

Stifled sexuality provided more than an assurance of chaste brides. It fitted into a social philosophy that extended into all aspects of domestic and working life, especially for the middle classes. If chastity was merely a matter of containment until marriage, with sensuality emerging full-blown in the conjugal realm, men might waste their potency in physical indulgence rather than devoting it to the progress of the nation. This would be dangerous for maintaining self-discipline, seriously disrupting the "spermatic economy" that channeled all energy into work.[6] Self-control for both sexes was ingrained in adolescents as a personal lifetime mission. Asceticism was a way of life: frugality in matters of economy and sex, duty and sacrifice rather than indulgence. This creed would be challenged by the abundance and affluence that was to open up in the modern era.

Around the turn of the century, as the nation's concern for production began to shift toward a preoccupation with consumption, there was a parallel trend away from work toward leisure, away from sacrifice toward satisfaction, and a corresponding decline of sexual repression in favor of physical gratification. As we have seen, courtship activities changed during these years with the opening up of urban amusements and an increasing emphasis on excitement and allure. With the decline of the ascetic lifestyle that had provided a consistency for Victorian values, the notion of virginity until marriage was much more difficult to maintain. Moreover, with the more private and "coupled" social life for adolescents, lapses in sexual morality were likely to result.

Indeed, an increase in premarital sexual activity did occur during these years. The proportion of brides who were pregnant at marriage began to rise steadily in the late nineteenth century, continuing into the twentieth.[7] One study that compared groups of men and women born prior to 1890 and after 1910 found that a much larger proportion of those in the younger sample were not virgins when married. The sharpest increase in premarital sexual activity was among native white middle-class women.[8]

Because public discussion of sexual behavior, coinciding with the increasingly sensual images of media personalities, reached a new level in the 1920s, it has often been assumed that the "sexual revolution" began then. Taking actual behavior as the indicator, recent research has shown that the shift began much earlier, in the last three decades of the nineteenth century. All the same, the extent of the "revolution" is easily exaggerated, for the pattern of sexual activity in America has been one of ups and downs.[9] Moreover, as another study has pointed out, the evidence gathered statistically "relates to sexual behavior rather than sex mores,"[10] and there may well be a certain tension between the two. In other words, an increase in sexual activity may indicate a greater defiance of social norms rather than a change in the social norms themselves. The Lynds, for example, observed that despite a notable increase in premarital sexual experimentation, a "heavy taboo" against intercourse between unmarried persons was "as strong today [the twenties] as...forty years ago."[11] With such severe social condemnation, young people who indulged in premarital sex may have felt extremely guilty.

While virginity before marriage remained the ideal, new notions about marital sex emerged. As the home became geared more toward happiness than toward discipline, the enjoyment of conjugal relations purely for pleasure lost its former stigma. The writings of theorists such as Sigmund Freud and Havelock Ellis gained wide attention. Even if few people actually read their treatises, popularization of their ideas served to erode the Victorian concept that intercourse should be for procreation only. But in light of the deeply held codes of the nineteenth century, and especially the persistent taboo against premarital sexual experimentation, the shift toward physical pleasure in marriage was not a simple matter. It proved extremely difficult suddenly to shed a firm tradition of abstinence and restraint.

The increasing acceptance of sexual gratification for both spouses had many important effects. For one, it undoubtedly encouraged young people to marry, in order to ease their guilt over erotic feelings and actions and legitimize their sexual indulgence. This may have been a factor in the increased marriage rate, as well as the declining marriage age. Without ingrained self-control to build a lasting wall against sensuality, one recourse was to wed so that dangerous urges could be freely and legitimately expressed. Adolescent sex may have been more widespread, but it undoubtedly led to a great deal of self-condemnation. Even as late as the 1970s, a group of college students expressed this inner tension. The vast majority of those surveyed, both men and women, felt that premarital sex was immoral. And yet the majority of this same group of unmarried college students admitted to having had sexual relations. In effect, they disapproved of their own behavior.[12] If young people in the early twentieth century felt equally uneasy about illicit sexual indulgence, they might have been encouraged to marry so that their behavior would gain public—as well as personal—sanction.

Given the remarkable staying power of this sexual ethic, it is not surprising that the divorce proceedings reveal conflicts over premarital sex, even after the union was solemnized. This double standard did not suddenly wane with the onset of the "revolution in manners and morals" that began to affect public behavior during the early decades of the twentieth century. If anything, anxieties rose as more and more middle-class women entered the public arena of work as well as amusements. Fears of sexual chaos loomed larger as they mixed with men of all classes. As we have seen, reformers during the Progressive era, in Los Angeles as well as other urban centers, were preoccupied with lessening the dangers of this public mingling. They worked to "clean up" vice zones and uplift amusements, while also attempting to make the workplace safer and less exploitative. Whatever the reformers did, women continued to participate in public life, while simultaneously shedding much of the outward modesty that had characterized well-bred Victorian ladies. As it became more difficult to determine, by appearance and behavior, whether or not a single woman was "chaste," the obsession with adolescent virginity may have actually increased.

One case from Los Angeles in 1920 indicates the way in which uneasiness surrounding adolescent sexuality might lead to irrational outbursts. Homer O'Malley was a husband who was attracted to youthful sensuality. At the same time, he associated urban amusements with the ruination of women. His complicated emotions led him to vile, emotional explosions toward his pubescent daughter as well as toward his wife. Homer and Maud O'Malley married in Bates County, Mis-

souri, in 1901. By 1920 they had a fifteen-year-old daughter and
a thirteen-year-old son. Maud was suing Homer for divorce on
the grounds of adultery. Among her complaints, she claimed
that on one occasion their daughter requested money to "go to
the picture show," and the father replied, "You damned little
whore, all you want is to go whoring around like your mother,
and you are going to be as big a God damned whore as she is
before long." This reaction indicates a deep dichotomy in
Homer's mind. In his repulsion and disgust at his daughter's
innocent pleasures, he revealed his own passion for youthful
women. For he also told his young daughter that he was going
to visit a sixteen-year-old girl who was "better stuff" than her
mother—and he was gone for two weeks.

Homer O'Malley's own attraction for young girls must have
increased the intensity of his venom against his daughter. He
was drawn to adolescents and their budding womanhood; but
his social attitudes of domestic morality counterbalanced his
physical desires, resulting in deep ambivalence. This confusion
surfaced in profanity, as when he called his wife a "cock-
sucking s.o.b." and told his daughter, "Go fuck yourself, you
little whore." Clearly, Homer O'Malley's reaction was not
typical. But his attitude shows how a man drawn to the new
style, but disdainful of the women who displayed it, might
respond to urban amusements such as movies. His erotic desires were at odds with his morals; the women he found attractive were no better than "whores."[13]

Even in 1920, if wives actually participated in premarital
sex, they might suffer harsh condemnation or outright rejection by their mates. Mary Lund, for example, had the mis-
fortune to have "fallen" prior to wedlock. She had sexual
relations "under the promise of marriage" before she met her
husband, and told him about the incident so that he would not
be deceived. Although she had been a faithful wife, her husband never forgave her this moral lapse before marriage and
threatened to tell their son "what kind of a woman" his mother
was. He told her she was "the lowest woman I ever knew. . . . I
picked you up in the gutter and I will put you back where I
found you." Significantly, due to her sexual experience, he
associated her with the Mexicans whom he despised, accusing
her of being "worse than the women below the line."[14]

As can be seen in table 14, the number of cases involving

premarital sex was not large in any of the three samples. But keep in mind that the issue concerned events that took place prior to the marriage. The lack of bridal chastity did not constitute a legal ground for divorce. Thus it could only serve to justify a divorce complaint on another ground, or an annulment for fraud, which was relatively rare (see table 15).[15] We can probably assume that litigants would try to avoid bringing sexual matters to the court's attention. This may well have been the case, for the largest number of complaints about premarital sex came from New Jersey, where state interviewers questioned the spouses directly (see table 16). Again we find that in every case, the woman's conduct, not the man's, was the source of trouble. One typical conflict was that of Susan and Leroy Jones, a Protestant couple married in Hightstown in 1917, and separated the same day. According to Susan, who admitted her "indiscreetness" prior to marriage, her husband, a twenty-two-year-old dry cleaning apprentice, deserted her immediately after their marriage. "I tried to get him to return and live with me as I intended to live a straight and honest life." But her husband would have nothing to do with her. He wrote her in no uncertain terms:

Sue: I am endeavoring to find employment of some kind and as soon as I succeed and begin earning a little money, I will send you what I reasonably can. I wish hereby to notify you however once and for all that for reasons I consider sufficient I will not under any circumstances live with you as my wife. Respectfully, LeRoy R. Jones.[16]

Similarly, William A. Treacy, a Roman Catholic, had his marriage annulled when he learned that his eighteen-year-old Catholic bride was not a virgin. He charged her with fraud, for he married her "under full belief from her conduct and representations that she was a chaste woman."[17] In another annulment, Arthur Noack, a civil engineer, said that "by reason of his discovery [that his German wife had an illegitimate child before coming to America] his health has been shattered, his peace of mind and domestic happiness destroyed, and his condition is most wretched." His wife was no less miserable, as she wrote to her mother,

Dear mother, I have already bitterly regretted that I went to America, for duing the three years here I have had nothing but trouble. . . . Dear mother, you probably can imagine how

little I care for such life. I don't know yet what to do. I better
close now, because I cannot think any further. Best regards
to all of you, from your unhappy Alma.[18]

The New Jersey cases also included eight "shotgun" marriages, which were entered to legitimize premarital sex or the
child that resulted. One young woman left her husband because she had a "feeling of hatred toward him because he had
gotten her pregnant when they were both single." Married
when she was seventeen years old and he a year older, they
only remained together thirteen days.[19] This case was unique
in that the bride was the one who left; in all the others, the
unwilling husband deserted. One of these, a twenty-seven-
year-old machinist, confided to a friend, "Well, I don't want to
say anything against her or 'roast her' but I would never have
married her if my father had not compelled me to do so, and I
will never live with her again." His wrath extended to their
child; he threw the baby into a crib, nearly killing it.[20]

Elaine Gulick was another woman whose "lapse" changed
the course of her life. "I was a school girl at the time my
husband married me, and if I had remained single, I would
have graduated that year. I was a member of the choir; my
husband's sister was the organist." She had known the father
of her baby for many years, but when pregnancy led to marriage, he deserted her after two days. He was a carpenter, but
did not support his child; she was forced to leave the baby with
an uncle, quit school, and work in a woolen mill.[21]

Often it was the bride's parents who insisted upon the marriage. Charles Regner met eighteen-year-old Della when he
was a twenty-one-year-old barber. They met "at a ball in
Paterson" two years before they married. "About three nights
after I met her," explained Charles, "I had sexual intercourse
with her, voluntarily on her part, and this kept right up until
she was in the family way and her father had me arrested and
we were married in the county jail." Although Charles Regner
made an effort to establish a stable family, Della preferred a
more adventurous life. "I tried to get along with my wife, but
she did not seem willing to settle down, but would rather go out
nights and have a good time." This is not to say that she had no
remorse. On the contrary, she was plagued by shame and guilt.
"Oh! I am sick of you, and I can never, never live with you any
more. You know why you and I were married; don't bother

me; let me alone." According to the interviewer, when her
husband saw the type of life she was leading, he lost all affection for her and stopped trying to get her back. She, in turn,
said she was ashamed and could never face her family and
friends again.[22]

Intense pressures faced young people who experimented
with sex prior to marriage. If they were unlucky enough to get
caught, especially through pregnancy, the force of familial
shame, public ostracism, and legal coercion was likely to
weigh heavily upon them. Marriage might ensue; but it would
not necessarily last. Speaking for a number of reluctant bride-
grooms was Charles Foster, who married his bride Rubina
when he was in jail. Immediately after his release he left her,
saying, "Your people have done this but they can't make us
stay together."[23] Adolescent sex, then, had this contradictory
character: youths were allowed to be sexy, but not sexual.
Lapses in moral stringency might lead to severe guilt, or at
worst pregnancy and forced marriage. With premarital sex car-
rying such a heavy stigma, how would newly wedded couples
justify the transition into legitimate conjugal relations? A sinful
act one day was to be holy the next, merely through the ritual
of a cermony. Given this tension is it any wonder that
erotic passion was not always incorporated into marriage with
ease?

By the 1920s, sexual relations within marriage was still regarded as loathsome by some and as lofty by others. One way
to reconcile these conflicting views was to place sex in an
ethereal, almost sacred realm where desire and intercourse
would become elevated from common lust. This tendency is
evident in the earliest arguments for a more expressive sexual
life, even among the "radicals" of the nineteenth century. The
Clafin sisters, infamous for their adherence to free love,
claimed that they had no desire to "reduce the relations of the
sexes to common looseness."[24] Victoria Woodhull, while
creating rifts within the nineteenth-century feminist movement
over her attitudes toward sexual freedom, still wanted to ele-
vate carnal desire to a spiritual level. "This involves a whole
science and a fine art," she said in 1872. Ultimately, she
equated the elevation of sex with the coming of the millennium:

The despised parts of the body are to become what Jesus

was, the Savior conceived at Nazareth. The despised body,
and not the honored soul, must be the stone cut out of the
mountain that shall be the head of the corner, though now
rejected by the builders. . . . Let the sexual act become the
holiest act of life, and then the world will begin to be re-
generated, and not before.[25]

This theme was picked up and carried into the twentieth
century, when it gained advocacy beyond the radical and
rather eccentric fringe where it had remained previously. If not
completely sanctioned by the mainstream, the affirmation of
sexual pleasure for both sexes did at least find wide expression
in "respectable" circles. Moreover, in keeping with a culture
committed to progress, expertise, and technique, the method
of sex became an important and serious matter for study.
Although we are most familiar with the sex manuals that have
held best-seller status in the 1960s and 1970s, they had their
forerunners as early as the turn of the century. Perhaps the
best known and most widely read of these authors was the
English "sexologist," Havelock Ellis. According to Margaret
Sanger, he was the first major western advocate of erotic play,
teaching the "how-to" of lovemaking with a variety of novel
positions and experiments. Sexual techniques, as advocated
by Ellis and others, promised to bring fulfillment and marital
joy. But this new idealization of sex flourished side by side
with the traditional stance of sexual asceticism. In the words of
one historian,

It was perhaps as much tragic as ironic that one solution to
the bleakness of American life was to abolish anxiety by, in
effect, abolishing sex, while a much publicized alternate was
to make sex an androgynous deity, intercourse a kind of religious rite.[26]

In both stances, however, there was a consistency. Sex was to
remain devoid of lust, whether its purpose was procreation or
bliss.

Illustrating this ideology was Margaret Sanger, best known
for her leadership of the birth control movement. Contraception was undoubtedly the most explosive development to
challenge traditional mores, for it held the possibility of un-
leashing premarital sex. Nevertheless, even self-styled "radicals" like Sanger and Havelock Ellis kept discussion limited to

marital intercourse.[27] Aside from giving women control over their own procreative functions, one of Sanger's strongest arguments in favor of birth control was its potential for freeing conjugal relations from fears of unwanted pregnancy, promising the total blossoming of physical marital bliss. But Sanger was concerned primarily with women's vulnerability to unrestrained masculine passion and its toll of excessive childbearing—a concern which permeated her attitude toward sexuality. Throughout her life, she held a fierce antipathy to male lust. This was sparked initially as a child when she watched her mother weaken and die after eleven children—the fruit of her father's appetites.[28]

While Sanger urged women to become more sexually expressive and creative, she warned men to be careful, gentle, and sensitive to women's needs. She vehemently condemned the use of "brute force" upon women to obtain gratification. It is interesting to note that she was against the contraceptive techniques of abstinence and withdrawal, for the sole reason that those means were frustrating for the woman. She advocated sexual fulfillment, but wrote about it in a manner that almost failed to acknowledge the participation of a man. Sexual activity for women, she wrote, could be "a psychic and spiritual avenue of expression ... the energy enhancing their lives and increasing self-expression and self-development."[29]

Obviously, this attitude toward physical pleasure was full of confusion. Sex was glorious, but only within marriage—and only if spiritualized at that. Women who had maintained a stance of abstinence and guilt regarding sex were expected to change their feelings totally and immediately upon entering the conjugal union. This shift would be disorienting at best. The difficulty would be further heightened if the woman anticipated intercourse as something mystical, but still deplored physical aggression. If the reality of sexual intercourse proved disappointing, wives might turn to the divorce court in order to shed their ill-matched mates.

This path was paved by the earliest advocates of divorce reform in the latter part of the nineteenth century. True to Victorian ideals, they felt that the home must be a realm of purity and protection for virtuous wives. Proponents of liberalized divorce laws argued that pure women who were victimized by vulgar and brutal men needed a legitimate means of escape. For example, *Arena* magazine, a major vehicle of reform, vigorously urged the public to accept divorce as necessary for women who were trapped by "prostitution within the marriage bond." The journal's editor expressed this central idea in his efforts to gain for women the right to divorce:

> For generations, the Church and society have tacitly sanctioned prostitution when veiled by the respectability accorded them by the marriage ceremony, until we have fallen so low that men have come to imagine they can indulge in licentiousness and debauchery from which the instincts of the lower animals recoil. . . . Too often the wife has found herself in the embrace of a human gorilla.[30]

Clearly, male lust was one of the baser instincts to manifest itself in human form—indeed a left-over passion of brutes.

Although some reformers still argued along these lines in the early decades of the twentieth century, the trend shifted toward concern for marital happiness and the right of either partner—but especially the woman—to free herself from an unsatisfying union. Divorce was regarded as a means for women to gain independence from oppressive marriages, and the arguments were closely tied to the fight for women's rights. Given the fact that many of those who urged divorce, birth control, women's rights, and suffrage also generally advocated sexual gratification for wives, perhaps women who did not find themselves sexually fulfilled in marriage ultimately would seek a divorce.

The women in the 1920 samples came of age in the midst of the publicity surrounding awakened female sexuality. Yet many of these daughters of Victorians had been taught since childhood that sex was dangerous. They were told that male passion was something unmarried girls must avoid, and married women must endure. Moreover, even those who affirmed the alternative, that sex is a positive aspect of life for both men and women, generally framed sexual intimacy in an ethereal context, devoid of passion. Looking at testimonies of twentieth-century divorcees, we find a remarkable holdover of grievances that plagued their 1880s forebears.

Admittedly, the data on this subject is quantitatively sparse; it is, however, qualitatively convincing. Considering the extremely private nature of these conflicts, even a small amount of candor is remarkable. There was no ground for divorce that specifically related to sexual offenses between married persons. The only purely sexual grounds were adultery and venereal disease. Most California complaints involving conjugal relations fell under the category of "cruelty." In New Jersey, these issues usually supported "desertion" petitions. We might assume that for the sake of modesty or privacy, divorce litigants would prefer to keep the issue of sexual relations out of the public records, if possible. In numerous cases, however, the problem was evidently so relevant that it could not be avoided. (See table 14.)

The first observation discerned from these complaints is the wide variety of problems mentioned, indicating that there was no particular "formula" used to gain sympathy from the court. The complexity and diversity of cases in this category indicate that sex was a very real and serious problem in these marriages, and may well have been involved in many more divorces than we can ascertain from the records. For each couple who included sexual complaints in the proceedings, there may have been several others who preferred to keep this issue out of the legal arena.

One case in particular illustrates this likelihood. In Los Angeles in 1920, Harry Hilman sued his wife Caroline for divorce on the grounds of desertion. One would have no hint as to the issue underlying the desertion if it were not for a revealing letter that had been placed in the file. Harry Hilman had written to Caroline that he filed for divorce on the grounds of desertion because he "had to fix things so it would read right and we could get the cheapest divorce possible." The reason behind the desertion charge, however, was stated quite succinctly:

If you want to come up here and live with me, if you would agree to sleep with me and be a bit reasonable, you could have anything you wanted. I don't understand why it should hurt you, and the doctors are telling me the same thing, you could do it if you wanted to, but the trouble is you are working against yourself and the laws of nature. . . . Yours very sincerely, Harry Hilman.[31]

The Hilman case was, truthfully and legally, a case of desertion. But the desertion resulted from a very real sexual problem. Whether or not sexual gratification for women was becoming acceptable in the public realm of discussion, this

particular woman was not leaving her husband because he
was unable to fulfill her desires. She was unable to experience
sexual pleasure. Her antipathy to intercourse was so deep that
the act caused her physical pain. Although this woman may
have been an extreme example, her distaste for her husband's
advances was not unique. In spite of the emerging affirmation
of female sexuality, the 1920 divorce records reveal a strong
holdover of Victorian sensibilities in attitudes toward sex and
an adherence to the idea of the early divorce advocates that
women victimized by lust within marriage should seek legal
redress.

Abhorrence of male lust was one of the most common feelings expressed in sexual conflicts by divorcing wives in all
three samples. This issue did not wane between 1880 and 1920.
In fact, it was mentioned more often in the later samples.
Perhaps this reflects a greater willingness on the part of women
to discuss such a private matter. But it certainly suggests that
wives, at least those getting divorced, had not accepted
wholeheartedly the notion of sexual delights, even within marriage. As we have seen, women did indeed hold higher expectations for marital gratification in terms of money, fun, excitement, and amusements. But as for this most intimate part of
the husband-wife relationship, we see very little change in the
turn-of-the-century decades. In the 1920 samples from both
Los Angeles and New Jersey, conflicts surrounding conjugal
sex were quite similar to those of the 1880s. Women still accused their husbands of sexual abuse, and men still complained
about wives who refused to have "reasonable marital intercourse." Typical of remarks by the wives who felt victimized
were those of Sarah Gude, a Los Angeles woman who sued her
husband of seven years for divorce on the grounds of cruelty.
She claimed that he was "unnatural and inhuman in his demands for sexual intercourse, demanding intercourse practically every night, and sometimes twice in one night, and frequently during the day time when he was at home, or came
home for lunch, even when the plaintiff was unwell and the act
caused her great physical suffering." She was granted the divorce, plus forty dollars a month alimony.[32] Like several women in the 1880s sample, as well as a number of her contemporaries, this woman equated "unnatural and inhuman" sex with
frequency of intercourse, rather than with any particular act.

Similar was the case of Allastein Wordin, another Los

Angeles wife who was granted a divorce after one year of
marriage, because the "conduct of her husband in their marital
relations was of so grievous and disgusting a nature as to cause
the plaintiff to suffer great mental anguish therefrom and
nerve-wracking fear of his approach."[33] New Jersey wives who
complained of sexual abuse used equally strong terms in describing their fear and outrage. Edith Foster, for example, was
a manicurist married to a Public Service Company worker for
nine years before their separation. The couple had married
clandestinely when she was seventeen, and had two children.
Joseph Foster charged his wife with desertion; his mother said
that the wife "ran around" and forced her son to do all the
house-keeping. But in her cross-complaint, Edith claimed that
the desertion was constructive, for she "fled" to her parents'
house as a result of her husband's abuse. He "insisted upon
intemperate sexual intercourse. When it was impossible for her
to gratify him, he practiced depraved and degenerate acts
upon her, over her protest, and by main physical force, making
her submit, to the great peril of her weakened health and to her
inordinate disgust and loathing." Nevertheless, the husband
gained the divorce and custody of the children.[34]

Another New Jersey woman left her optician husband after
five years of marriage and one child. Aside from his adultery
"with a heavy set woman," he was guilty of sexual abuse from
the moment they married. On their wedding night, Ethel and
August Meister arrived in their appartment at 1:30 A.M., and
August said he was "so damn sorry he had married" her and
that he had done it only for sex. Ethel said he was "very brutal
in his treatment of me—he threw me on the bed and did that
thing four times. The next morning, he kept me in bed until
11:00, and twice that morning did the same thing." Over the
years of their marriage, "he just used me as a tool. At night, he
would turn me around and do what he wanted and turn me
right back over again, and not come near me or anything else at
any other time. He didn't even consider a woman's time when
she shouldn't be touched. Twice a night was very little
and often three times a night. I protested to him and his answer
was 'What are you here for?'" To make matters worse, "he
always carried four absolutely rotten pictures of nude women.
They were disgusting. He would show them to me, he would
look at them, and in about ten minutes he would want me to go

to bed. He was nothing short of an animal." This couple married young, when the husband was twenty and his bride seventeen. Perhaps the restraints put upon young people prior to marriage contributed to their problems. She was never able to adjust to his desires, and he was insensitive to his wife's feelings, and perhaps resentful that he had to marry her in order to sleep with her. Ethel Meister won her suit and was restored to her maiden name.[35]

It is worth noting that the women in all three samples who complained of sexual abuse were inclined to use powerful and emotionally loaded adjectives such as "inhuman" or "unnatural" rather than detailed descriptions of specific acts. Those who did reveal the nature of the abuse usually alluded to frequency of intercourse or oral sex. Most comments were similar to those of Helen Mall, who claimed that her sixty-five-year-old physician husband of seventeen years was "lewd and unnatural in his sexual desires and habits . . . forced her to have unnatural intercourse with him . . . told her on numerous occasions that he only cared to live with her to gratify his sexual desires."[36] These were powerful statements, but devoid of specifics. Judges rarely felt compelled to request details, expecially if the husband defaulted. But in cases where the men gave their side of the story, we often find a great deal of misunderstanding surrounding the issue, indicating that sexual incompatibility stemmed largely from conflicting ideas as to what constituted normal marital relations. The extent of "reasonable marital intercourse" seems to have become a matter of some disagreement.

The 1920 case of Mary and Paul Pflager illustrates this problem. After eleven years of marriage, Mary accused her husband of sexual brutality, saying that he "attempted to and by the use of physical force and violence did commit upon the body of the plaintiff acts of sexual depravity and degeneracy so revolting as to be improper of expression or description." She was, continued the complaint,

a delicate woman in poor health, and is unable to earn her own living because of a nervous breakdown suffered as a result of husband's acts. . . . Plaintiff's health has been affected, she is in such nervous condition that the presence of defendant when he comes to visit child causes great fear and suffering lest defendant again attempt to practice said acts on plaintiff.

This testimony suggests visions of horrible sexual brutality, but the situation appeared entirely different from her husband's perspective. He simply claimed that his wife had "willfully and persistently refused to have reasonable matrimonial intercourse." Although there may well have been exaggerations on both sides, it is possible that both partners, from their own viewpoints, were telling the truth. The court was sympathetic to the wife, however, and granted her the divorce, custody of their child, and ninety dollars a month alimony.[37]

A common theme in these proceedings was the wives' distaste for aggressive passion on the part of their husbands. In one interesting case, two potentially rival women held a bond of sympathy in their feelings of abuse. The petition was filed for bigamy by Nellie Wilson, whose husband, William, had told her that his first wife was dead. When Nellie discovered that the first wife was indeed alive and still legally married to William, she filed for an annulment. At one point the first wife wrote the younger woman a rather sympathetic letter, gently letting her know that she had been deceived on many levels and also expressing some feelings that might have been shared by both wives. She wrote that William was in fact fifty-five years old, not forty-three as he told his twenty-one-year-old bride. "You say you was a good young Christian woman, why ruin your life with an old man? I was not twenty when I married him, my father tried to get me to let him go but I wouldn't listen to him." Expressing pity for the young woman, she added, "Does he Bull and pant at you yet if he don't he sure has changed wonderfully." Nellie was granted the annulment.[38]

While women accused their spouses of sexual abuse, men were likely to complain about their wives' conjugal stinginess. Austin Hemon, for example, divorced Florence, a New Jersey wife who wanted no sex at all. Her frustrated husband finally sued for divorce after ten years of marriage, six of which they spent living together. According to Austin, their trouble was caused by Florence's "refusal to act the part of a wife. She refused to have sex." Although she "had a slight operation which enabled her to" and the doctor said the "best thing for her was to bear children," she still resisted, saying only that she "would be committing sin against herself and against God to bear children by me."

Finally Florence called a minister to act as an arbitrator. But when the clergyman told her that the Bible instructed wives to submit to their husbands, she became enraged. After he left, she told her husband that the Reverend "was no different from any other man. . . . All men were brutes, all men were selfish, and that all men wanted was to gratify their passions, and that was about all the use men had for women." She told Austin to "get a divorce and go to the devil," she would "never consent to have children by such a pup" as he was. In spite of his frustration, Austin still upheld Florence as a model of true womanhood. "I want to say this with regard to my wife, that as far as her personal character is concerned, there can be nothing said against her. She is absolutely one of the finest girls there could be, outside of her temper. Morally, she is as fine a woman as ever lived. I cannot speak highly enough of her chacter in this respect." She just did not like sex.[39]

Not all divorcing wives in 1920 were so averse to conjugal intercourse. A significant number of women in the sample were seeking sexual fulfillment and rejecting the stifling mores of the past. While few in number, they are an important departure, for there were hardly any who expressed similar desires in the 1880s. We also find that, among divorcing men, this sexual awakening on the part of their women was not always pleasing. In fact, several husbands found sexual passion in a wife quite disturbing. (See table 14.)

If women associated male lust with "brutes," men regarded passionate women as "whores." The double standard had enforced a code whereby men might gratify their appetites with women of the "lower orders"—not those suitable for marriage. For urban men during the turn-of-the-century decades, this meant immigrants, blacks, and "lower-class" ethnics. Consequently, if a "respectable" woman showed eagerness for sexual pleasure, her mate might consider her shameless, and on a par with those despised groups who had served as a sexual outlet for middle-class men—in fancy if not in fact.[40] This association is revealed in a number of divorce cases.

One husband expressed disgust toward his wife's sexual desires, which were thwarted by his impotence. Aware of his own inability to satisfy her passionate nature, he linked her with the group commonly considered most sensual: blacks. Hazel Holland sued her husband James for divorce because he was "physically unable to enter into the marriage state . . .

"impotent." She claimed that he knew of his condition before
they married but failed to tell her, and that it was incurable.
Moreover, her husband was brutal and vulgar, calling her a
"God damn whore" and accusing her of "whoring around and
staying out at night." Significantly, he told her she was "no
good.... You are sleeping with niggers and I hope you get a
dose of syphilis and cannot walk." He continually referred to
her as a "damned nigger lover," insisting, "You run around
with niggers."

Whether or not there was any truth to James Holland's accusations, the assumption is clear. His wife's sexual desires
placed her in a category with "niggers" and "whores." What
is interesting, however, is that notions of class and respectability were also used by the wife to account for her husband's conduct. He was an oil wagon driver, while she considered herself a "refined, educated and cultured woman, and a
graduate from San Francisco normal school and has taught
music and is now playing a pipe organ in a large theater in Los
Angeles, and has been reared and cultured in a refined environment." Beyond her husband's impotence, she accused him
of "vulgar and vile and angry language, general annoyance and
abuse." Testifying as a witness, the wife's mother was even
more explicit as to her son-in-law's inferior status. Her
daughter, a "musician, organist, piano teacher," married a
"teamster, that is all I know." As such, he was "uncouth,
ignorant, and brutal, and treated her like a dog." This wife
declined in class in the eyes of her husband, due to his perceptions of her sexuality. The husband in turn was scorned by his
wife and her family due to his inferior status. In court, James
defaulted, and Hazel was granted a divorce plus thirty dollars a
month alimony.[41]

Although attitudes expressed by the litigants often associated sexual passion with the "lower" classes, ethnic
minorities and immigrants, the cases do not indicate any basis
in fact for these assumptions. As the data in table 16 show,
working-class men complained of "prudish" wives as often as
white-collar men, and blue-collar wives were just as likely as
their middle-class counterparts to complain of sexual abuse.
Women with allegedly passionate natures were also evenly divided among socioeconomic levels. If these sparse statistics
indicate any class differentiation, it is in the frequency of sexual complaints rather than the complaints themselves. Sexual

conflicts in general were mentioned slightly more often in blue-collar divorces. This may reflect a greater willingness to discuss the matter than among more genteel white-collar couples, rather than any proclivity for working-class couples to have sexual difficulties.[42]

Some men were deeply suspicious of wives who showed sexual inclinations. One such husband was William Burnett, who married Mina in 1913 when he was a twenty-one-year-old carpenter and she a girl of sixteen. Judging form the complex accusations, it appears that Mina was flirtatious at best and promiscuous at worst. But according to her husband, she was a "lewd and dissolute person . . . mentally deficient in regard to the sexual relations." She, however, claimed that her husband not only failed to provide adequately for her and their baby, but was guilty of an "inhuman" assault upon her. Both partners, in this case, considered the other somehow sexually depraved.[43]

Sexual obsessions occasionally became rooted in fantasies directed toward a spouse. Alexander and Dora Loren had been married for twenty years. Dora complained that her husband accused her of having sexual relations "with men and boys ranging from fifteen years to almost decrepitude," saying she was a "damn whore" and a "son of a bitch." She charged him with calling her a "dope fiend" and the mistress of all the boys who had come to visit their daughter. She also charged that he never bought her any clothes. Fantasies may have been involved on both sides, however, for Alexander countered the last charge by submitting as evidence bills that he paid totalling $250 to fashionable department stores, all in 1917. Nevertheless, he confessed to his wife's other complaints, and she won her suit with a property settlement.[44]

Considering the emotional tangles that could result from tensions surrounding sex, it is no wonder that we find some divorce cases involving frustrations which led to perversions. Although some of the accusations in this category were quite obviously exaggerated, a number of the atrocities mentioned clearly were not imagined. One case in particular illustrates the sordid extremes to which a man might resort to overcome a wife's conjugal reluctance. Mary Krinian sued her husband Harry, an immigrant elevator operator, for divorce on the grounds of neglect and cruelty. She claimed that he was guilty of "foul and vicious accusations" and "boastful and taunting confessions," telling her he had intercourse with her insane mother. A letter from her husband supported the wife's charge; but the motive is as remarkable as the incest. In the midst of several ominous threats as to her fate in the hereafter, he wrote, "The Lord is going to show you if I love you or not also the children. . . . My heavenly father will testify against all you done to me." He admitted having had sexual intercourse with her mother, but indicated that he had a definite purpose in so doing: "I had lots of reasons for doing it, to perhaps help you to gladly fulfill my demands on you." Astonishingly, it seemed to have had the desired effect, for he wrote, "It did help a little and you had forgiven for it." Mary Krinian was granted the divorce, custody, and property.[45]

Wives who were sexually frustrated had no similar recourse. They could not force themselves upon unwilling mates, nor resort to the peculiar tactics of a man like Harry Krinian. But those women who did feel unfulfilled displayed no hesitation in discussing the matter once they brought it to court. They considered their charges valid and legitimate. One case reveals the wife's adherence to the ideal of sublime sex, for she complained, ironically, of both abuse and lack of gratification. Irene Antel had married in 1914 when she was a clerk of eighteen and her husband a twenty-two-year-old bricklayer. She said he refused to have "reasonable and natural" intercourse with her, and that "from three to five times a week, except on occasions when she was unable to have sexual intercourse by reason of illness, the defendant has insisted upon having and has had incomplete and unsatisfying sexual intercourse with the plaintiff, and . . . has caused a severe shock to her nervous system and a serious and permanent impairment of her health, and has caused grievous bodily injury and mental suffering." She was granted the divorce, plus five dollars a week, and half their jointly owned automobile.[46]

The most fully articulated expression of sexual liberation came from Rose Macman, a radical woman from New York. She and her husband were both twenty-two-year-old middle-class Jews when they married in 1917. He was a lawyer, and she a schoolteacher. After one year of marriage they separated, and divorced in New Jersey in 1920. When Norman Macman tried to get his wife back, she wrote him,

There is nothing doing, your efforts are hopeless. I have lost all affection for you, in fact I never had very much. You know that I am not the kind to live with a man because I am married to him or because the law says I am his wife. I believe I can live with whomsoever I please at any time provided I have sufficient love for him and I have no love for you. All is over between us. You do not fit my ideal of a man.

Norman further explained, "My wife has always been radically inclined and I firmly believe she is an athiest and never believed in the institution of marriage." He related a conversation they had, in which she revealed her ideological distance from the American mainstream: "Marriage to me is not something that is sacred. . . . You know that I am an athiest and we athiests don't believe in any vows." Then "why did you marry me?" Norman queried. "I knew you would not cohabit with any woman before being married." "Do you mean to say that when you stop loving a man you won't live with him?" "If I loved a man, I would live with him, even without being married to him." Rose Macman may have been in the vanguard of the sexual revolution, but in spite of her radical philosophies, she remained bourgeois in her aspirations: "To tell you the truth, I don't care if I go back with any man, nor would I go back with you for the simple reason that you cannot support me the way I want you to. You are of that slow conservative kind, the way all lawyers are." Oddly enough, she still wanted to be supported by her husband—and in a somewhat regal fashion. She was a teacher herself, but her "athiesm" cost her her job.[47]

With the exception of Rose Macman and a few other women with acknowledged sensual natures, we find that divorcing wives in the 1920 sample resembled their Victorian mothers more than the dominant image of the "new woman." But a fundamental change in attitudes toward sex within marriage had occurred in American culture. By the turn of the century, the shift away from asceticism was well under way, and acceptance of sexual pleasure was spreading to more members of the society. It was not merely radical thinkers or popular enthusiasts who expressed these ideas. Indeed, by the 1920s, even the Protestant churches, among the most conservative social institutions, had accepted the importance of sexual fulfillment in maintaining marital stability. Sex, the religious leaders claimed, could help cultivate "spiritual values" within families.[48]

Profound as this shift may have been, it was not complete. For sex prior to marriage was still considered sinful, and within marriage it was elevated to a level of mystical euphoria. Lust, so fiercely condemned by the Victorians, was hardly more tolerated by the new advocates of "spiritualized sex." For young people in the society, this meant an almost certain crisis, at some point, during their years of maturation. Early sexual instincts had to be suppressed vigorously throughout adolescence, to prevent "falling" prior to marriage. Within wedlock, intercourse was to be pure and ethereal, devoid of baser "animal" passions. Given this impossible stance, it is no wonder that sexual conflicts appeared among divorcing couples.

The double standard was alive and well in 1920, wreaking havoc in many marriages. Men and women both adhered to the tacit assumption that single men could experiment sexually with "loose" women, but brides had to be chaste. Combining these contrary experiences in marriage was no easy task. In general, women seemed to have had more difficulty adjusting to marital sex. This is understandable, for the unyielding insistence on premarital purity condemned them to naïveté. While young men were often out in the world and becoming somewhat experienced prior to marriage, girls usually remained sheltered in their parents' homes. Although not publicly sanctioned, it was generally expected that men were to have some sexual encounters prior to marriage. But for young women to do so meant "ruin," for virginity still marked the line between "good" and "bad" girls.

A woman's early training was geared to marriage. She was to attract men by cultivating an alluring style that promised sexuality. With women's lives limited in all other spheres, this quest took on overwhelming importance. But ironically, the courtship period was to remain absolutely chaste as a prerequisite for a sexually gratifying marriage. With the deep conflicts and ambiguities surrounding sexuality, it is no wonder that many couples were unable to integrate sexual pleasure into their married lives. For most divorcing men and women in 1920, the "sexual revolution" was still a long way off.

Seven

Wives at Work

If sex was not the answer for anxious urbanites in search of fulfillment, perhaps engaging occupations would absorb their restlessness. This had been a traditional solution for men, but now women, too, could look to the economic arena. In the early decades of the twentieth century, new job opportunities for women abounded. If domestic life seemed confining or unsatisfying, perhaps economic endeavors in the public realm would provide the excitement women craved. This was indeed the belief of feminists, who felt that emancipation should bring women out beyond the walls of the home. Without rejecting the ideal of marriage and family life, a feminist like Charlotte Perkins Gilman could argue,

Yes, most girls marry. All girls ought to—unless there is something wrong with them. But . . . if the girl had a few years of practical experience in the world she would be far better able to enjoy and appreciate her own home when she had one. . . . For the home's sake, as well as for her own sake, the girl will profit by experience in the working world.[1]

Not everyone agreed with Gilman. In this as in other sectors of life, traditional assumptions die hard. But nothing did more to shake the foundations of Victorianism than the influx of women into the labor force. Working women posed a direct challenge to the traditional sex roles which had provided the basis for domestic life. As one Victorian described the code, "[The] woman who could not make a home, like the man who could not support one, was condemned and not tacitly."[2] Men made the money; women tended the household. Any deviation from this formula threatened the entire fabric of the social order, which rested on the centrality of the family. But as more and more women went to work, the sharp separation that had

divided the sexes in the nineteenth century began to break
down. Perhaps this was the key to modern marital happiness: a
union of equals, both working, both returning to the home for
relaxation and leisure. Whether or not this would indeed be the
case, the possibility generated a storm of controversy.

For feminists like Gilman, a job offered an opportunity for
self-improvement and personal experience away from the
home. But for more traditional thinkers, the new economic
opportunities seemed to threaten not only what was best in
women, but the very moral fiber of the nation. According to
one of the most influential antagonists of women's emancipation, Edward Bok, editor of the *Ladies Home Journal,* not
only have women "shown themselves naturally incompetent
to fill a great many of the business positions which they have
sought to occupy," but it has been to their detriment:

It has certainly done the health of women no good; on the
contrary, it has filled our rest cures, sanitariums, and hospi-
tals to the doors. It has been an unnatural condition of
affairs.[3]

Bok was a self-proclaimed conservative, but he shared many
beliefs with the reformers. Although Progressives were the
strongest advocates of extending women's domain into politics
and the economy, even liberal thinkers faced these issues with
ambivalence. In a remarkable memoir, appropriately entitled
The Confessions of a Reformer, Frederic Howe explained this
dilemma: "My beliefs about women were far deeper hidden in
my mind than were even the moralities of the Church." He had
married a college-educated feminist who wanted economic
independence. While he rationally agreed with her position on
women's rights, it "destroyed my sense of masculine power,
of noblesse oblige, of generosity." A working wife was, ultimately, "a public admission of failure by the husband." De-
siring his "old fashioned picture of a wife" to "serve" him, he
resisted her desire to work. His efforts on behalf of the feminist
cause were at best half-hearted:

I spoke for women's rights without much liking it. My mind
gave way, but not my instincts. . . . And I sometimes doubted
whether many of the men who spoke and worked for the
equality of women really desired it. . . . They clung, as I did,
to their propertied instinct, to economic supremacy.[4]

If this was the uncertain stance of one of the more committed advocates of women's rights, what of the ordinary men and women in the society without reformist inclinations, who had been reared to judge a man according to his ability to provide? And what was the qualitative nature of these new and threatening options for women?

The most rapidly expanding occupations for women were those on the lower levels of the white-collar hierarchy: stenographers, secretaries, sales personnel, and clerks. These were not the only jobs opening up, however, nor were they the most numerous. At the turn of the century, over one million women were engaged in the mechanical and manufacturing industries, three times the number in those occupations thirty years earlier. The increases in domestic and personal services were even higher. But the professions, with the exception of nursing and teaching, were still overwhelmingly male, as were the positions of power or leadership in businesses and corporations. In spite of the rapid increase in the female labor force, few women ended up in prestigious or lucrative occupations.

As it was difficult to combine the demands of a lifetime career with the duties of homemaking, most professional women remained unmarried, as had been the case in the nineteenth century. In fact, most working women in all occupations were single, and relinquished their jobs when they married.[5] The percentage of married women who held jobs, however, practically doubled in the first three decades of the twentieth century, from 6 percent to 11 percent.[6] This proportional increase was not matched until the 1940s. But it is wise to keep in mind the opposite implications of these statistics: that as late as 1930, nearly 90 percent of all American wives remained out of the work force. Marriage was still the main career for women. Thus the startling increase in working wives, noticeable as it was, actually affected a very small segment of the married female population. Given this situation, those who feared the destruction of the family due to increasing job opportunities for women appear to have been alarmists. After all, a working wife might supplement the family income; but rare was the employed woman—either married or single—who really could maintain economic independence. In most cases, a woman's earnings would provide a meager existence at best.

Very few women, then, were engaged in rewarding and financially secure jobs. Most were probably subject to an even worse routine than the majority of men, lacking the same possibilities for security, advancement, or adequate income. Like most men, they worked primarily for the pay check, anticipating time off the job when they could reap their rewards. Single working women may have looked forward to marriage and quitting the job. But it is not clear how those who were married felt about their work. The Lynds found that white-collar as well as blue-collar wives who worked did so for the money. Often, they were content with the arrangement. The work experience itself was not necessarily exciting, but the extra contribution to the family budget was welcomed. In fact, the Lynds found that both men and women worked primarily for off-the-job pecuniary gains:

For both the working and business class, no other accompaniment of getting a living approaches in importance the money received for their work. It is more this future, instrumental aspect of work, rather than the intrinsic satisfactions involved, that keeps Middletown working so hard.[7]

Given these realities, the public debate over the inherent value of jobs for women must have seemed irrelevant to many of those who worked. While the controversy remained limited to a small, articulate group of prominent individuals, the issue reached far into the lives of ordinary people. Employment for women was a fact to be confronted, beyond the point of analyzing its merits. Many, if not most, worked out of necessity, rather than choice. Since their jobs were usually underpaid, low-skilled, and monotonous, it is not likely that work in itself was particularly rewarding. Contrary to the assumptions of many women's rights advocates, "emancipation" was not necessarily to be found in the workplace—especially under demeaning, discriminatory, or boring conditions. Approached from the standpoint of those who were employed, the question of whether or not women should work was beside the point. What, we must ask, was the quality of their work experience and how did it affect their family lives?

Looking at the divorce cases from 1920, we find that the wife's job was a frequent source of conflict. Clearly, many women fully expected marriage to mean freedom from employment. Let us look at the jobs these working women held.

As was true of the 1880s sample, working wives appear to be somewhat overrepresented among the litigants, relative to their proportion of the population. (See table 6.) In the Los Angeles sample from 1920, 41 percent of the wives had worked. This figure is slightly ambiguous because many of the occupations were taken from marriage license records, which do not indicate whether or not the woman continued to work during her marriage. It is also likely that some of the jobs mentioned were held only after the couple separated. These are serious problems; but it is still a large proportion, for in 1920 only 28 percent of Los Angeles women over the age of twenty, married or single, were employed. In the 1920 New Jersey sample, 42 percent of the wives held jobs, compared to 24 percent of the women in the state. Clearly, work was more common among divorcing women than the married female population as a whole.

There are several obvious explanations for this over-representation of divorcing women in the workforce. A certain sense of financial security derived from the job may have en-couraged unhappily married working wives to seek a divorce. Some may have even taken the job in anticipation of being on their own. Others, perhaps, may have enjoyed the sense of independence that employment provided. But the cases them-selves strongly suggest that satisfaction with the job was not a major reason for seeking divorce. In fact, discontent with work was one of the most common complaints present in the sam-ples. To understand this high degree of malaise, we must con-sider the types of jobs the divorcing women held. As tables 8 and 17 indicate, working wives in the 1880s sample from Los Angeles were largely petty proprietors and laborers, while none were listed as clerks and secretaries. In the 1920 Los Angeles sample, however, there were more white-collar than blue-collar women listed among the litigants, with the largest numbers falling into the lower ranks of the corporate bureau-cracies. The rest remained concentrated in those occupations that had always contained many women. In other words, the categories of independent businesswomen and blue-collar workers shrank as the clerical ranks began to expand. In New Jersey in 1920, the situation was somewhat different. The majority of wives listed as working held blue-collar jobs. (See table 18.) Perhaps there were more blue-collar jobs for women in New Jersey due to the highly industrialized nature of the state, while the corporate bureaucracies may have been growing more rapidly in Los Angeles, where there was less manufacturing.

The statistics take on deeper significance when comparing the women's jobs to the men's. (See tables 8, 17 and 18.) The higher percentage of professionals among wives in the 1920 Los Angeles sample is due to the occupations of teaching and nursing, fields traditionally dominated by women. On the bottom rung, there was approximately the same proportion of women as men in lower-blue-collar jobs, the women mainly as domestics, the men as laborers. In New Jersey, working women were even more heavily concentrated in blue-collar positions than their husbands. Like their nondivorcing counterparts in the work force, most of the women in all three samples were not participating in economic endeavors previously restricted to men. In fact, among the traditionally all-male professions and business elites, we find very few women.

These working wives, like employed women in general, entered the economy in large numbers, but not in positions of power or potential lifetime careers. The significant fact about those in the sample, then, is not that their occupations were particularly rewarding or lucrative, but rather that so many of them had worked. In order to determine the effects of employment on their marriages, we must go beyond the work experience and probe their attitudes. Financial independence might have made it easier for a woman to go through with a divorce, but we do not know whether the job itself was directly related to marital difficulties. Were these wives satisfied with their work outside the home? Did they choose to pursue their jobs at the expense of marriage? Did they want economic independence?

Fortunately, the testimony of these women provides direct evidence of strong attitudes about their jobs. Among the wives who expressed their feelings on the matter, we find a rather remarkable degree of discontent with their working lives. As we learn from table 7, divorcees in 1920 were hardly more enthusiastic about their jobs than their 1880s counterparts. Out of 206 employed Los Angeles divorcing wives in 1920, 90 claimed that their husbands did not adequately provide for their needs, and 37 asserted that they were forced to work against their will. In New Jersey, where the vast majority of employed wives held blue-collar positions, fully 66 percent complained that they did not want to work.[8] Rather than welcoming a chance for some economic independence, most of these 1920 litigants expected their husbands to provide for them. If women's rights meant a job, they wanted no part of it. In fact, "emancipation" may have suggested freedom *from* work rather than freedom *to* work.

Why, then, did these women work? The 1920 divorcees, along with most other people in the workforce, seemed to be working primarily for money. Like wives in the 1880s sample, many did not want to work, and condemned their husbands for failing to provide adequately for their needs. Blue-collar women in particular accused their husbands of forcing them to take a job, and none indicated any reason for working other than financial need. It is not surprising, then, that working-class couples were torn apart by the causes as well as the effects of the wife's job.

The Treadwells, for example, married in Salt Lake City in 1912, where they remained until 1917. At that time, Isaac Treadwell moved to Los Angeles, planning to obtain work and send money for his wife, Elizabeth, to join him. According to Isaac, Elizabeth refused to come to Los Angeles even when he sent for her. But she claimed that he never sent her any money; and in fact she stayed in Utah in order to work and send *him* money. Curiously, both spouses in this case seemed to be displeased with the wife's occupation. Elizabeth's husband was a mail carrier; she worked as a hotel chambermaid. Although they had no children to compel her to remain at home, and he admitted that his wife earned a decent salary, he "objected to her doing that kind of labor." She did not particularly enjoy doing it, either. When a deputy wrote to Elizabeth, asking if she would be willing to return to Isaac, she replied,

Yes, whenever he gives me satisfactory assurance that he will treat me in the future as a husband should treat his wife, pay my lawyer fees, advance me $50 as part payment on my expenses since he left . . . and provide for me in the future.

Obviously, economic independence was not what Elizabeth Treadwell wanted. There is no indication that she ever came to

Los Angeles. But Isaac, apparently, did not return to her. In 1921, he was still working as a mail carrier in Los Angeles. Although the case was never resolved, the couple probably remained separated, without an official divorce.[9]

Isaac Treadwell was not the only working-class husband who felt ambivalent about his wife's job. Although men generally preferred their wives to remain at home, financial pressures often prompted them to urge spouses to work. Edwin and Verona Rich were plagued by problems revolving around Verona's job. The couple married in Kansas City in 1910, lived together for eight years, and had one daughter. In her complaints of cruelty, Verona claimed that after their child was born, Edwin forced her to take a job, saying, "You are just as able to work as I am." He then left her and went to California, telling her to stay and keep her job. In 1914 he sent for her to join him in Los Angeles, but by the time she arrived he had left for Santa Barbara. Finally in 1915 she followed him, and he found her a job as a hotel chambermaid, again forcing her to leave their child with strangers. Although he earned eighteen dollars a week at the time, he took part of her wages. When they returned to Los Angeles, she first worked as a menial, then found employment at the Film Exchange, which was the first postion she enjoyed.

Just as Verona found a job she wanted to keep, however, war broke out and Edwin made her quit and become totally dependent upon him, so that he would be exempt from the draft. When the war ended, he again told her to get work. But he refused to give her any money while she looked for a job, remarking, "You are a good looker and if you can't do it any other way you can go out with other men." To add insult to injury over her unwanted employment, he got angry when she purchased a hat with the money she earned working in a cafeteria. For some reason, the case was ultimately dismissed. But there is no evidence to suggest that the couple ever reconciled.[10]

These sorts of difficulties appear in the New Jersey proceedings as frequently as in Los Angeles. This is especially noteworthy, since "neglect to provide" was not a legal ground for divorce in New Jersey, as it was in California. In other words, women who complained that they were forced to work mentioned it incidentally, since all petitions had to rest on a

charge of adultery or desertion. Obviously, these statements
were not made merely to fit a legal formula. Many women
expressed their anger and frustration at having to work and
contribute to the family income. Some chafed when husbands
insisted on their help in small businesses. Janet Golden, for
example, was forced to work in her husband's bakery. She
complained that the work was too hard, she had to get up
early, and she "did not want to be in business at all." Her
bitterness ran so deep that she swore if she ever saw her husband lying in the gutter, she would not so much as give him a
glass of water.[11] Similarly, Amy Robinson hated helping her
husband in his saloon. Finally she just packed up and left, "to
be free and do as she pleased."[12]

Clearly, these wives were not enthralled with their work.
Yet it was working-class men and proprietors of small businesses who were most economically insecure. Feeling severe
financial pressures, they often resented the obligation of being
the sole provider. Frank Willis "did not think he ought to be
obliged to support his wife, simply because he married
her. . . . She could get out and get a job as well as he could."
Spencer Tritus, a molder on his second marriage, agreed, saying, "A man is a fool to work for another man's daughter."
Eric Ronsaville, a woodworker, summed up this feeling when
he told his wife to "paddle her own canoe." Harold Holden, a
New Jersey laborer, went so far as to tell his wife she could
"get money like any woman who wanted to get money."[13]

Although most of the above cases involved people with limited means, even affluent couples often quarreled over whether
or not the wife should contribute to the family income. Norton
Walters, for example, earned a good profit from his business as
a produce broker. But among the issues that dissolved the
Walters' marriage was his insistence that his wife, Claire, also
ought to work. The couple married in a Roman Catholic cere-
mony in 1912, in New York City, when Norton was twenty-
nine years old and Claire was twenty. They had one child and
separated after five years. Norton announced that he would
"never rest until he drove her from the house." As long as she
contributed nothing to the family upkeep, she was merely
being tolerated and had nothing to say about household matters. Yet his ambivalence and guilt surfaced in a vague but
loving letter he wrote her in 1915, asking her to give him a

chance to reform. "We've had some wonderful times, dear, and with a long life ahead of us, things in general should be all we desire, and you can help so much in making my dreams come true. I'm asking you for one chance to prove that I'm all you thought I was three short years ago." Apparently, the one chance did not work out, and they separated two years later. Claire was granted the divorce, plus the return of her maiden name, custody, and the remarkably large sum of sixty dollars a week for the support of their child.[14]

These cases from Los Angeles and New Jersey in 1920 suggest that in spite of increased job opportunities for women, the legal system reinforced the notion that the husband must be the sole provider. Not one case out of all that were examined indicated that the courts sanctioned a husband's plea for a wife's financial contribution. There is even some evidence to suggest that a woman was justified in marrying specifically for money—although "love" was supposed to be the only legitimate reason to wed. The divorce of Sadie and Harry Marcus is a case in point. They both were Russian immigrants who married in Los Angeles in 1917 when Sadie was a thirty-one-year-old divorcee with four children and Harry a thirty-eight-year-old tailor. After four months they separated, and the following year Sadie sued for divorce on the grounds of fraud. She claimed that Harry married her on the agreement that he would support her and her children so that she would no longer have to work. He promised he would start his own tailoring business, or support them on his forty-dollar-a-week earnings. When his promise proved false, she was forced to put her children in an orphan home and work to support them. Harry defaulted, and Sadie won her suit.[15]

The problem of work was obviously more complicated for women with children, like Sadie Marcus. Mary Oreb also had a child and was anxious to remarry and gain financial security. She had married Peter Oreb in San Francisco in 1910, and they had a seven-year-old son at the time of their divorce. Peter made three hundred dollars a month at his saloon business in San Francisco; he deserted her there in 1917. Mary also claimed that he was habitually intemperate, and failed to provide for her. She requested custody, fifty dollars a month alimony, one hundred dollars in court fees, and twenty-five dollars a month child support. Although Peter never appeared in court, a witness upheld Mary's charges, saying that the saloon owner continually "took the pledge and broke it again." The court granted her a divorce by default, along with fifty dollars a month. In 1921, Mary claimed that her ex-husband owed her fourteen hundred dollars past alimony. But in 1923 Peter answered that Mary had remarried and left for New York. As evidence, he enclosed a letter dated 1921 in which she wrote, "I am sure you would rather see me happy and well supported than compelled to work for wages that couldn't support either Jack [their son] or I. . . . My ambition is to see him go to college and get a good start in life." In response, the court relieved Peter of alimony payments, but he still was required to support his child, with $32.50 a month.[16]

The 1920 divorce proceedings both from Los Angeles and New Jersey indicate an overwhelming concern with the husband's duty as provider and the wife's desire to be supported without working. In this respect, the later litigants resembled their 1880s predecessors who unequivocally opposed work for married women. By 1920, however, the issue had become more complicated. Not only had the notion of jobs for women gained wider public acceptance, but more and more individual women expressed a strong desire to work. We find this trend reflected in the divorce samples. Although most of the wives wanted their husbands to support them, a significant minority desired employment and appreciated their freedom and independence. Their numbers, however, were limited to a small group of white-collar women. Looking closely at these cases, we find that the employment experience itself was rarely the prime motivation for working.

If blue-collar women worked out of financial need, white-collar wives often took jobs that provided enough economic autonomy to allow some freedom from their husbands. Edith Taylor, for example, deserted her husband, William, a hardwood finisher, after ten years of marriage and two children. Edith was enjoying her new life, but apparently it was the relief from her troublesome marriage, rather than her job per se, that gave her the most satisfaction. She wrote to her husband that there was no use trying to get back together again:

We just can't get along, fuss and quarrel all the time, and I am to [sic] used to making my own money now to ever settle down to housekeeping. I have had more than a year of freedom now, and I have been happy, and I intend to live my own life, in my own way. . . . Glad to tell you I am in the best of health, hoping you are the same, I am, your wife Mrs. Edith Taylor.[17]

This woman, in spite of the fact that she had two young children, welcomed the opportunity to manage her own affairs. We do not know how her husband felt about her job, but Edith implied that he tried to convince her to give up her employment and return to him. Where husbands did express attitudes toward wives who wanted to work, we find a great deal of discomfort and uneasiness. An employed wife was, essentially, a woman with a life at least partially removed from the home. Unlike nineteenth-century voluntary activities for middle-class women, a job was not seen as an extension of their traditional role. Nor could it be placed in the context of overall family and community betterment. As we have seen, reformers as well as so-called "conservatives" feared that as women entered the economy, the home would collapse. Presumably, since they would no longer "need" men for support, their economic as well as leisure pursuits would lead to sexual chaos.

These fears are revealed in many of the later divorce cases, especially those involving middle-class women who wanted to work, without being forced to take jobs out of dire financial need. (See table 7.) Helen Armstrong, for example, was a New Jersey woman who sought employment in order to earn money that could purchase her freedom from the home. She and William Armstrong married in 1911 in Burlington county, New Jersey. This Protestant couple had no children and divorced after seven years. The New Jersey state interviewer concluded that Helen had lost all affection for her husband William, and was "desirous of having a good time and more money." According to William, all their troubles began when Helen went to work. His testimony is so revealing that it deserves to be quoted at length:

We lived happily together for more than five years and she never made any complaint of my treatment of her, but about the time the War broke out my sisters were working and making good wages and my wife expressed a desire to earn more money for herself in commercial work. It was not exactly satisfactory to me, but I made no objections except to tell her that I preferred for her to remain at home. She did go to work at Dreers Nursery at office work. She had all the money she made for her own clothing and saved considerable. She did not work regularly but when she got a good supply of clothing and ready money on hand she would quit for a while. As she became acquainted with young people at work, she frequently expressed the desire for more money and better times. Then she left. . . . I can give no reason why she left unless it was her desire to get at the large wages which she would earn at office work and she might have tired of me in some ways although I never gave her any cause to be dissatisfied with my treatment of her. My wife was a poor girl when I married her and I outfitted and supplied her with all her needs and practically never refused her anything in the way of clothes or support. The only reason I can give for her wanting to leave is that she desired to have a good time and thought if she were separated from me, she could enjoy herself better.

In this remarkable statement, William Armstrong articulated the consequences he believed to have resulted from his wife's job. Because she earned her own spending money and associated with a new group of people at work, she began to carve out a life for herself beyond the domestic confines. Finally she left the home altogether. Helen was drawn to a life outside the home that seemed more exciting than that of the dependent housewife. As William's sister testified, "She said to me several times that she did not intend to go to housekeeping or to be tied down by domestic life and that she preferred to have a good time and could do it better by doing office work and getting her own money. She frequently went to the movies, but when I asked her about them, it was obvious she had not attended the movies at all or had paid no attention to the pictures if she had. I think she left to have a free foot, good times and more spending money."[18]

A number of husbands agreed with William Armstrong and preferred to have sacrificed and struggled to provide for their spouses rather than risk the possible consequences of the wives' independent means. James Ford, for example, implored his working wife to give up her job and return to him: "I have done everything within my power to provide properly for you; in fact, the home and surroundings I have given you have really been above my income and it has often imposed personal hardship upon me to make this provision for you." Violet Ford, however, did not relish the idea of becoming totally dependent upon her insurance broker husband. Choosing to keep her trade as a furrier, she wrote to him bluntly, "I can't live with you. Violet."[19]

In the Ford and Armstrong cases, the wives had occupations which enabled them to support themselves adequately. We have no evidence to indicate that the job was the sole reason for the divorce; but clearly their incomes made it possible for these women to strike out on their own. In both cases, the husbands were not happy about the wives working and urged them to give up their employment, letting the men be the sole providers. Both husbands' comments suggest that their pride was also involved. They struggled to provide for their wives and to keep them dependent at home. Nevertheless, these women preferred at least a modicum of independence. If the man refused to tolerate any autonomy for the wife, the woman may have felt inclined to discard her husband rather than her job.

This was indeed the case with Henry and Lisa Douglas. Henry was so offended and humiliated by his wife's desire to work that he deserted her after only three months of marriage. This Protestant couple married in Trenton in 1915, when Henry was a twenty-four-year-old automobile driver and display man. Lisa explained that he was violently opposed to her working to pay off debts: "He was insulted to think I would so disgrace his name by going to work, and that was why he left me. . . . He considered it incompatible with his dignity to have me work. He said, 'I am not going to stand any more of this, if you are going to disgrace my name by working, I am not going to stay here.'" He left, and Lisa was granted a divorce with the restoration of her maiden name.[20]

Henry Douglas obviously felt that a working wife was an affront to his masculine pride, which fed upon having a dependent spouse. Other husbands, however, allowed their wives to work, only to regret it later when they believed it led to marital problems. Perhaps the most telling case is that of a New Jersey couple, Mae and Harold Atweis. Their marriage had many difficulties to begin with, but when Mae began working, the relationship totally fell apart. This childless couple lived together five years after their Jersey City wedding. Harold Atweis earned thirty four dollars a week, probably as a white-collar employee. Mae was twenty-one years

old when they married, and later took a job under her maiden
name as a sales department solicitor. When Harold asked Mae
to give up her job and "make a home for him," she refused and
went home to her parents. He then filed for a divorce on the
grounds of desertion, explaining that Mae's job was the main
sore spot between them. "We had arguments about her work.
She went to business all week and did her housework on
Saturday and Sundays and it was not to my satisfaction." Like
many men married to working wives, it never occurred to
Harold (or to Mae, for that matter) that if both spouses
worked, both ought to contribute to the housekeeping chores.
Mae was still expected to perform her domestic duties on a
daily basis. Nevertheless, Harold tried several times to save
the marriage. "For yours as well as my sake," he implored,
"give me *a man's chance* to set things right." But Mae did not
yield. Finally, he wrote again, revealing his exasperation—
along with his resentment against her job:

My dear Mae, In my opinion you have been influenced
otherwise and you see fit to ignore everything, even your
marriage vows, which, outside of entering the Church, are the
most sacred a person can take. If I had mistreated you in any
way or had done anything a husband had ought not to have
done, there would be an excuse for your action. Ever since I
have been married, I have tried to please you, have stood any
number of things that most men would not have stood. Have
tried to do my best to succeed in business and have suc-
ceeded in raising myself to my present standing. This never
would have been so if I had not thought of my wife and
looked forward to the future, where we could have a home to
ourselves with all the enjoyments that go with a good home.
Stop and think. The majority of young fellows are not making
the salary I am and they have families to support.

After this exposition on his worthiness, Harold began to lash
out at his wife and her independent career:

You claim to have paid for the furniture. How long have you
been going to business? How many fellows would have stood
for their wives doing what you have been doing [using her
maiden name]? If a husband could allow that, it shows a spirit
of trust for the wife. How many trips did you make to Canada
when you ought to have been by my side? How often have I
spent every last cent on you, for your benefit?

Finally he reached the crux of the issue, where all of his fears, resentments, and wounded pride came together:

I made a big mistake in allowing you to go to business. It has made you feel quite independent. Also, associating with people that are not worthy of your notice. Girls that think it is real smart to talk of things pertaining to married life and intimacy with married men. These have made a great change in the girl I married for love. . . . I leave the next step to you with a gentle reminder that I endeavored three times to make you understand that with you and you only I was ready to unite again. . . . Before closing, Mae, let me say you have always been a good wife and a good housekeeper and could be a good mother if you wanted to. It seems my hopes have all been shattered and I am alone on a great dessert.There is nothing so great as the loss of a loved one. With sincere love, your husband Harold.''

In a postscript he asked for the keys to his trunk, which was the only part of his long letter that sparked Mae to reply. Unmoved, she sent him a brief note: "Friend Harold, Your trunk is ready as you requested, enclosed is key. Kindly send for your trunk before Thursday as we are moving. . . . Friend Mae." With this terse end to their troublesome union, Harold Atweis obtained a divorce.[21]

This distraught husband objected to many aspects of his wife's job. He felt she was getting too "independent." She associated with the wrong kind of people at work, presumably fast women with questionable morals who had a bad influence upon her. And, not the least of his annoyances, her work kept her from tending to the home. In his mind, he had been overindulgent with his wife by permitting her so many out-of-home activities. Her independence triggered his fears of all the worst possibilities: sexual freedom and the neglect of wifely duties, leading to the collapse of the moral home. Two similar cases from Los Angeles suggest how other husbands of working wives might become irritated with their wives' neglect of household duties. The final result, they felt, was sexual immorality.

Luella and James Howland were married in San Diego in 1904, had no children, and lived together until 1918 when James deserted. Luella claimed that James neglected to provide, although they were obviously quite affluent. According to Luella, they held a great deal of community property, including several lots, furniture, and an automobile, with a total value of $23,000. She requested half of the property, plus alimony. James responded by denying the charge of neglect; in fact, his wife had been a self-supporting real estate broker since 1915:

Since the entry . . . into her business and occupation she has failed and refused to perform her duties as the wife of the defendant, and has insisted upon devoting her time and energies to her said business and occupation to the exclusion of the performance of her duties as the wife of the defendant.

He also claimed that she became "careless in housekeeping and refused to cook and wash dishes, would lie awake nights scolding at him or reading magazines, and then would refuse to arise in the morning and prepare breakfast or attend to any housework." Implying a causal relationship, he further accused her of adultery, at the "Historic Sycamore Tree" in Sawtelle. James also requested a divorce, plus division of the property. While denying all charges, Luella expressed frustration at her husband's condescending attitude toward her. She said that James always criticized her management of business and household matters and made "sarcastic reflection . . . upon her limited schooling and education." Nevertheless, the divorce was granted to James, on his cross-complaint charge of adultery. Luella remained in Los Angeles pursuing her real estate business.[22]

The charges on both sides may have been essentially true. What is interesting is the way in which James Howland associated his wife's job with her entire degeneration. Because of her business, she became argumentative, slothful, lazy, and neglectful of her household chores. Ultimately, it led to her adultery. But perhaps James was unable to perceive in Luella's actions a rebellion against his overweaning sense of superiority.

Another case involving many of the same issues was that of Bert and Lisa James. When they married in Los Angeles, both were twenty-seven years old, and Lisa had been divorced once before. Bert was a stock salesman from Arkansas; Lisa was a market cashier from New York. They had an infant son. Bert filed the initial complaint on the grounds of cruelty, claiming that "though he was able to and did properly support her, she insisted upon leaving her home and working." The result, he argued, was her subsequent neglect of household duties, followed by moral and sexual laxity. Lisa would not "cook his meals for him and failed and refused to properly or otherwise perform her household duties." She soon "used intoxicating liquors" and began going out every night against his wishes, getting angry if he objected. After their son was born, she moved back to her parents' home; and he had not been able to see his child since. He requested a divorce, plus custody of the baby.

Lisa James replied by denying all the charges, claiming that her husband did not "properly support her," and that she worked "according to an agreement they made before marriage, that she would continue her job." She filed a cross-complaint on the grounds of cruelty against her husband. Similar to James Howland, Bert James was obsessed with his own sense of dominance. He told Laura that "he was vastly superior to her in mental and intellectual powers, that she was a fool and a child, that her ideas were absurd, foolish and ridiculous, that he would uplift her to be his mental equal, that she could not be blamed considering the poor material of her parents who didn't amount to anything." Once he grabbed a religious periodical that she was reading while riding a streetcar, saying, "Put that away, don't be so cheap as to try to make a display of your religion in public." On another occasion, on the way home from a Christian Science church meeting, Lisa criticized a speaker and her husband exploded: "You contemptible little fool; you ought to be killed for criticizing a Christian Science meeting." He would even question her on minor and mundane issues such as the price of salad dressing she purchased. Displeased, he told her she "could not be trusted to buy any more things for the house. . . . Everything that came into the house thereafter would be bought by him." He even went so far as to throw her on the ground, yelling that he was "boss" and she was "cheap and no good . . . infinitely beneath him." Adding insult to injury, he remarked that he did her and her family a great honor by marrying her.

This couple never did see eye-to-eye. Lisa claimed that the only reason she worked was to support herself and her child, since Bert neglected to provide for them. She requested a divorce, custody, alimony, and court fees. In reply, Bert claimed that Lisa never wanted a baby, did not want to be bothered with it, hated housekeeping, and wanted to return to her former job at the market as soon as she could. He believed that she only went to her parents to relieve her of the care of the child, although he had offered to support the infant. This long and messy case was finally resolved when the court granted the divorce to Lisa, plus custody and fifteen dollars a week. But that was not the end of it. In 1926 Bert requested custody, saying his former wife "ran around" and was an unfit mother. He claimed that he had a nice big house with a sixty-year-old housekeeper "of great refinement and culture" and lived in a "very fine residential section." He also wanted the child placed in a private school, under his care. In this case, bitterness remained long after the divorce. The record ends with a new trial pending over the issue of custody.[23]

These cases reveal many severe problems that might surface in marital conflicts, often involving the wife's job but resting on issues that ran much deeper. Luella Howland and Lisa James worked. Both husbands opposed their wives' employment, claiming that the women neglected their household chores and became morally as well as intellectually unfit. Although neither wife expressed feelings about the work experience itself, they claimed that their husbands considered them inferior subordinates, lacking intelligence and the ability to manage their own affairs. With these attitudes and the husbands' apparent need to keep their wives totally dependent, it is not surprising that these women insisted upon working. However, we have no indication that they were particularly involved in their jobs or preferred financial independence. In fact, they both complained that their husbands did not adequately support them. For these two women and perhaps others in similar situations, the job may have been primarily a way for them to prove themselves capable of something other than housework—and to get out from under the dominance of their husbands.

Only one divorcing wife displayed eagerness for the work experience itself. The case of Lillian Kohler is quite interesting because out of the more than twelve hundred proceedings examined, she was the only woman who gave any indication of enthusiasm for her career possibilities per se. Others expressed satisfaction with their financial rewards or with the diversion from household chores or freedom from the husband that work provided; but only Lillian Kohler really seemed to

enjoy the endeavor in which she was engaged. She and
Franklin Kohler were married in Hoboken, New Jersey, in
1911, and divorced in Los Angeles in 1920. They remained
together until Lillian deserted in 1916. Her husband was an
electrical engineer; they had no children. Shortly after their
separation, Lillian wrote Franklin a warm and friendly letter,
wishing him a happy birthday, and expressing a desire to continue their friendship, although "fate has decreed for us to go
our separate ways." She was studying journalism at a university, hoping to get a job working for "*Women's Wear,* a New
York commercial paper for manufacturers in the East, to keep
them in touch with women's needs in every large city." If she
was not able to get that position, she planned to "sell bonds for
a reputable bond house as the young men are being substituted
by women on account of the War." She sent her fondest
wishes, and signed, "Lovingly, Lillian." Franklin was granted
the divorce on the grounds of desertion, by default.[24]

These cases involving women who expressed an interest in
work have been quoted at length because they show the various and complex ways in which the issue of a working wife
contributed to marital difficulties. But it is important to keep in
mind that these women were in the minority, and that every
wife who wanted to work—for whatever reason—held a
white-collar position. Also, in almost every case, the husband
was a lower-white-collar salaried employee, or a blue-collar
worker, torn by the conflicting pressures of financial strain and
masculine pride.

Obviously, a marriage in which both spouses worked was
not necessarily doomed to fail. But these particular cases
suggest that many unions collapsed because the couples were
unable to integrate the wife's job into marital harmony.
Numerous husbands of working women had not transcended
Victorian assumptions in the slightest degree. Many believed
that if a wife went to work, she was exposed to bad influences
which could lead to sexual immorality. Moreover, she would
neglect her household chores, and the home would fall apart.
And on top of it all, her husband would suffer the stigma and
humiliation of having a working wife—an affront to his dignity.

Similarly, most of the women in the divorce samples appeared to be less than eager to hold jobs once they married.
They hoped that wedlock would free them from the need to

work, and resented husbands who forced them to take jobs, through neglect or otherwise. But even the few wives in the samples who did want to work suggest a complex array of motives. Many hoped to gain some financial security, which would allow them to be less dependent upon husbands who felt they were incapable of anything other than household drudgery and subordination. Others hoped to earn enough money to buy things that their husbands could not or would not supply. Still others simply enjoyed the freedom from the home, and may have used the job as the first step toward shedding a stifling marriage. What stands out in all these cases is that very few women wanted to work for the sake of the work experience itself.

At first glance, it appears that these women were rooted to the past, frightfully dependent and no more "emancipated" than their Victorian forebears. But this cursory judgement may be quite unfair. The wives in the 1920 samples were part of a generation of restless women who were reaching out, justifiably, for new horizons beyond the confining modes of the past. If they displayed little enthusiasm for the work world, it was not because they did not try. As we have seen, their jobs were limited and monotonous, offering little hope for excitement or long-term possibilities for advancement. Given such options, the women in the samples who had no desire to work were not simply lazy or selfish. Discontent with their jobs and desire for financial security in marriage must be examined in light of their experiences.

Charlotte Perkins Gilman may have spoken for a very small segment of housewives when she argued that if a woman had

eight hours of specialized work, to be done with and left with eagerness for the beloved home, she would have a far fresher and more stimulating mind than she has after her ceaseless, confusing toils in the confined domestic sphere.[25]

Gilman's idea was sound, but sadly ahead of her time and out of tune with existing circumstances in the economy. At the time that she wrote, most jobs available to women were not attractive alternatives to housekeeping. The problem was not with her genuine feminist principles, but rather with the limitations inherent in the work world. Without fundamental changes in the industrial system, Gilman's advice would seem irrelevant to many working women. More applicable than Gilman's words might have been the ironic and naive statement of Judge George Bartlett:

I certainly do think a wife ought to work.... A job keeps a woman out of mischief; improves her health, and gives her an interest in the home that many otherwise do not have. Most of all it helps use up her excess energy, which I believe causes more ruction than we realize in a lot of homes. The man comes home tired after his day at the office and the wife is full of pep. What's the result? She thinks he's getting to be an old crab, and he thinks that she is losing her mind.[26]

Bartlett's notion was hardly a viable solution for women's restlessness. It is no wonder that they began turning back to the private side of life with renewed eagerness.

Eight
The Pressure to Provide

In spite of the influx of women into the workforce, the Victorian assumption that a woman should make a home and a man should provide for one still held strong in the America of 1920. But something had indeed transpired since the nineteenth century: the Victorian synthesis had begun to crumble. Women were breaking out of former roles. The workforce, however, did not adequately absorb their new restlessness. In order to carve out a more satisfying existence, they turned with heightened expectations to the private sphere of life. The problem, however, was not easily resolved. For as the standard of living continued to rise and desires for a consumer-oriented lifestyle intensified, families would need to keep pace either through two salaries or through the provider's ability to satisfy increased demands. Since neither men nor women were eager for wives to go to work, it fell to the husbands to supply the needs for this modern domestic universe.

The divorce samples reflect this trend. During the years between 1880 and 1920, issues surrounding money—who should make it, how much is adequate, and how it should be spent—became increasingly prevalent. Although the percentage of cases actually filed on the grounds of "neglect to provide" did not rise significantly between the two samples taken (see table 15), these problems did become more complicated in the later decades. The Lynds found a similar development in Muncie, Indiana. In spite of the fairly constant rate of neglect complaints in divorce litigations from 1890 to the 1920s, "economic considerations figure possibly more drastically than formerly as factors in divorce."[1]

At first glance, this appears rather perplexing. The nation was more prosperous in the later period than earlier, and the standard of living was rising steadily for all classes. Women,

Portions of this chapter are adapted from an earlier version published in the *Journal of Social History* 12, no. 2 (1978).

moreover, found greater opportunities to work, and, together
with men, experienced increasing wages and more free time off
the job. At the same time, an unprecendented abundance of
consumer goods became available on a mass level. Presumably, these developments would contribute to easing tensions
between husbands and wives rather than creating them, while
fostering a more pleasant and comfortable existence. With
the standard of living rising, however, and affluence filtering
down to a greater proportion of the population, the husband
was often expected to meet the increased demands sparked by
widespread prosperity. In an era of mass consumer goods,
what constituted the "necessities of life"?

One judge saw this dilemma as a major element in marital
break-ups: "Modern couples are money conscious, whether
rich or poor." Judge George Bartlett, writing his memoirs in
1931, looked back on his twenty years as a Reno divorce court
judge and gave his advice on every pertinent subject from
sex to money. Concerning financial matters, he revealed a tremendous ambivalence. On the one hand, he hailed the new
affluence:

It really makes little difference, save in degree, whether the
American father makes $300 or $30,000 a year. His children
ride in an automobile, play the radio and Victrola, and go to
the movies.

On the other hand, he was aware that prosperity could "com-
plicate the problems of modern marriage for the paradoxical
reason that our needs diversify with our blessings."[2]

Indeed, Madison Avenue spared no energy in order to "diversify" the public's "needs." Department stores, catalog
houses, and numerous shops and salesrooms put new products
within the reach of the masses. Shopping became a major
pastime for American consumers. Between 1870 and 1900, the
number of persons involved in the distribution of goods grew
from 850,000 to 2,870,000; and the proportion of the national
income derived from trade rose from 12 to 18 percent. As
Edward Kirkland has pointed out,

Celebrated as American thrift was, the growth of trade implied that Americans had a propensity to spend as well as to
save. . . . There were no historic social taboos limiting the
purchasing aspirations of the masses. For the humble as well

as the exalted, comfort and even luxury were possible—if one
had the price.

Given this new proclivity to spend, the stakes became higher
for the husband-provider, for, as Kirkland continues, "A standard of living also depends upon what people think they ought
to have . . . in terms of services and commodities."[3]

By the turn of the century, advertising played an important
role in raising the level of demand for goods and encouraging
spending. A New York agency in 1893 wrote that advertising
"is a more powerful element in human progress than steam or
electricity."[4] As it was women who had the most time to shop,
advertisements were geared increasingly to them and the market for domestic items. Shopping could become a major preoccupation, if not an obsession. Judge Bartlett warned his
young male readers,

Money to a woman has an altogether different connotation
than it does to a man. . . . He has worked for it; she has, in a
sense, given herself to him partly for the privilege of sharing
what he has.[5]

Bartlett took the argument so far as to imply that purchasing
was something innate to females. To illustrate, he related a
woman's alleged response when he asked, "Don't you miss
shopping?" Although she was supposedly "a working woman
who loves her job," her reaction was a sad one:

The lady's smile disappeared. A wistful look crossed her
face "I miss a lot of things," she admitted, still looking down
into the street where women shoppers were hurrying up
and down. "Silly things, I guess. But I miss them—
probably because I'm a woman after all."[6]

If Judge Bartlett did not totally invent this story, he undoubtedly exaggerated shamefully. But the message is clear: the
potential for disappointment increased in the early twentieth
century when a modicum of luxury became the anticipated
norm.

Women were bombarded by media messages telling them it
was their right to expect both leisure and affluence from their
mates. Even young single girls were taught, before being carried away by "the first handsome fellow who comes along," to

take a good glance at his wallet. "Fie and shame on the im-
provident beauties... who fall in love... and lose their
hearts... without first looking up his financial standing."[7]
Once married, men were no longer urged to devote their energies and resources to the nation's progress, coming home
merely for peaceful refreshment and the edifying influence of
their wives. They were now expected to return with cash in
their pockets, ready to use it and their nonworking hours to
make their women happy. This new expectation was one major
aspect of the expansion of consumption and leisure in the
domestic sphere. While women looked to the home for a
greater sense of meaning and fulfillment, the burden of acquir-
ing the trappings of this domestic life fell to the providers.

As we have seen, in the 1880s there was no controversy over
what constituted the necessities of life. Either a man provided
for his family, or he did not. By 1920, however, it was no
longer clear precisely what constituted adequate support on
the part of a husband, and a number of bitter conflicts erupted
over the issue. These difficulties were not limited to couples
with inadequate resources. Money problems affected marriages of the wealthy as well as the poor. (See table 19.)

The Keagys, for example, were an affluent Los Angeles
couple who lived together only seven months. John Keagy was
a dentist with a good deal of property, and his wife Zella was
also fairly wealthy in her own right. According to John, Zella
had a monthly income of seventy-five dollars (although he does
not say from what), plus six lots in Alabama, bank accounts,
stocks, and diamonds. She was married previously, and had a
daughter. The evidence suggests that she was widowed,
although that is not entirely clear. Apparently, John and Zella
had a rather stormy relationship. Throughout their charges and
counter charges of cruelty, humiliation, violence, and insult,
they had a running debate over financial matters. Zella felt
neglected. She complained to a friend that John "did not appreciate her enough, she didn't like the house he furnished her,
that her house in Alabama was so fine, and that her first
husband would have sacrificed anything for her." She requested a divorce, five hundred dollars in fees, and seventy
five dollars a month alimony. Denying the charges, John filed a
cross-complaint on the grounds of cruelty, claiming that Zella
"proceeded to run bills against him, without justification,

which were not for the necessities of life." Finally Zella was granted a divorce, and the bitter financial conflict ended with a property agreement. In this case, money may not have been the primary issue; but it certainly aggravated an already bad marriage. In spite of their wealth, John and Zella Keagy could not agree on an appropriate level of expenditure.[8]

Another example suggests how a wife's material desires might put strains upon a marriage, if a husband's income was adequate but not enormous. Edward and Louise Atkinson were a middle-class couple who married in Brooklyn in 1910. During their ten-year marriage, they spent several years living apart and had constant quarrels over money matters. Finally Edward filed for a divorce. Aside from Louise's alleged adultery, her husband claimed that she "spent money freely and extravagantly and with utter disregard of his circumstances." Although they had no children, he gave her his thirty-five dollars a week salary, keeping only one dollar to buy tobacco and other small items for himself. From 1915 to 1917 she remained in New York, refusing to join him in California. At the same time, she corresponded with other men who gave her money.

One "bone of contention" between the two was Louise's fetish for pet dogs. Edward objected to the dogs, not only because of their expense, but because of his wife's obsessive doting upon them. He complained that her pets "would constantly lick her and put their tongues in her mouth and sleep in bed with her," to his unmitigated digust. When he protested, she said that "her dogs could do more for her than he could," for she loved them and hated him. Although Louise never appeared in court, Edward submitted some of her letters as evidence. In one, she asked him for seventy-five dollars for another dog, which she "would rather have than an evening gown"—implying that she would go without one "necessity" for a pet. She also complained of the sacrifices she had made for her negligent husband: "I sold Peggy [a dog] to buy you a suit." In another letter she claimed that he owed her money, for "there is no Tom [reference unclear, perhaps her lover] here to take care of me, and I am not well enough to work."

Edward Atkinson considered his wife's material desires quite outrageous. But apparently she found a paramour who was more inclined to cater to her tastes for the trappings of elegance and high culture. He wrote her slick letters about fancy hotels where she could stay on New York's Fifth Avenue, learn painting "from a good teacher and meet artistic people," and frequent his luxurious new club house which was "most comfortable in every way." At the same time, she wrote to her husband in California that she was in a dire situation:

Now, I am in need, do I have to make out an itemized bill, or do you have enough *manhood* to do the proper and decent thing towards me.

According to Louise, this meant "weekly payments until such time as you figure you have done your duty." She then told him to go ahead with the divorce, she will not object. The court apparently had no sympathy for her alleged difficulties, and granted Edward the divorce. Nevertheless, Louise's pleas are revealing. Not only did she consider herself "in need," but she equated her husband's ability to provide for her desires—however eccentric—with his very "manhood." For Louise Atkinson, manhood and duty were equated with taking care of women—and in the proper style.[9]

This equation reflected more than the demand of an outraged wife. It symbolized a much larger social attitude that had evolved with the maturation of industrial society. While public notice focused on women's changing activities, parallel shifts that affected men went virtually unnoticed. Men continued to work, their clothing styles remained practically unaltered, and their public behavior did not change dramatically. Yet they were experiencing a subtle transformation in sex-role expectations which, while not as obvious as the new status of women, was no less profound.

For white-collar men, the most far-reaching changes came with the maturation of the corporate system. The engulfing bureaucracies stabilized many uncertainties of the earlier era and offered at least a modicum of security. The twentieth-century businessman was less likely to enter business on his own, with the full burden of success or failure resting on his shoulders. If one followed the rules, one would advance up the hierarchy in a steady, predictable manner, and reach a moderate level of success and prosperity. There may have been few examples of men making a fortune overnight within the modern system, but in fact the Carnegies of the previous era served as little more than encouragement to fantasy. The top of the ladder was almost impossible to reach then as well as later. The giants of the nineteenth century were obsolete as models of successful striving. In spite of new rewards, the corporation took away some of the unique triumphs of individual enterprise.[10]

With the mechanization of industry, increasing production, the declining work week, and a rising standard of living, the benefits of the corporate system were obvious. In terms of purely material considerations, such an economy offered abundance and leisure. The tragedy, however, was that the aspiration for affluence was more widespread than the luxurious life itself. Even if an individual entered the white-collar ranks, he still faced enormous pressures to advance and succeed. Supplying increased demands necessitated continual striving. This was difficult enough for relatively successful businessmen, but infinitely more so for employees with modest salaries.

We know from national statistics that the white-collar level of society shifted away from self-employed petty proprietors to corporate bureaucrats and clerical workers. The samples reflect a similar trend (see tables 8, 16 and 18). These white-collar groups, possibly more than any other level in society, were striving for upward mobility, afraid of "slipping" down the socio-economic ladder, and concerned with deriving the fruits of their labor in tangible material goods. Entrepreneurs facing competition from large corporations, as well as rank-and-file white-collar workers, may well have felt these pressures most intensely.[11] Looking at the divorce samples from Los Angeles, we find that in both periods, the low-white-collar level is overrepresented, compared to its proportion of the general population (see tables 8 and 17). In the later sample, the category of independent petty proprietors shrank dramatically as the more bureaucratic clerical and sales categories mushroomed. Those who remained among the entrepreneurial ranks felt new pressures. As large chains and department stores began drawing local patrons and customers away from independent enterprises, owners of small shops and businesses may have felt increasing insecurity. Those who tried to cut costs by turning to family labor often faced resentful wives, as some of the cases in the previous chapter suggest. It is perhaps no wonder that this group had more than its share of divorce.

Fortunately, some of the divorce litigants articulated how financial and status considerations affected their marriages and their lives. In terms of material considerations, we are able to discern a pattern of discontent for each of the major socioeconomic levels represented.[12] As we saw in the cases cited above, affluence did not preclude the possibility of money squabbles (see table 19). The leisured wife of a man with means might make a quasi-career out of purchasing goods and adorning herself and her abode. Even wealthy husbands may have reacted against frivolous or wasteful expenditures. But if a man's income was consistently a measure below his wife's aspirations for comfortable living, the tension could become chronic and destroy a marriage that otherwise might have survived.

In the divorce proceedings, conflicts over status and social mobility stand out in bold relief, particularly among white-collar families on the west coast. It is here that we can best perceive the intensified pressures placed upon men to satisfy heightened material desires. Norman Shinner, for example, admitted that he deserted his wife after five years of marriage because of his "inability to support her in a manner she desired on my salary, and on this account we could not live together in an amiable manner." Rather than struggling to meet up to his wife's aspirations, Norman Shinner simply left.[13]

Oscar Lishnog faced similar difficulties. He married Martha in Chicago in 1908, and had four children prior to their Los Angeles divorce. While the Lishnogs appeared to be a fairly comfortable suburban family, financial strain ultimately caused their union to collapse. Oscar was in the insurance and real estate business, working as an employee or salesman rather than executive or proprietor. His income was steady but modest. He spent some time living apart from his family while working in San Pedro, exchanging frequent loving, chatty, but slightly distant letters with his wife. He sent her money, she tried to save, and they expressed affection for one another. Now and then Martha would tell Oscar to "mind the store and not waste time or money." Revealing her material aspirations, she wrote that many of her neighbors owned automobiles, for there was no street car line nearby. This suggests that their Los

Angeles home was in a fairly new suburban development, removed from the downtown district and transportation network. Martha also reminded her husband that she was paying mortgage on the house, and the "kids want a hammock." She usually closed with affection, saying she was "waiting for him."

But in 1920, Martha filed for divorce on the grounds of willful neglect, saying that Oscar spent his thirty-five dollars a week salary in "riotous living away from his family," squandering his money while depriving his wife and children. Claiming that she was not skilled in any vocation, Martha said she had to rely on the charity of friends. She asked for custody of the children. Oscar denied the charges, insisting that he earned only twenty-one dollars a week and gave it all to his wife except a small amount for living expenses. He asked that the divorce be denied, and assuming that they would remain living apart, requested joint custody of the children. Nevertheless, the court granted Martha the divorce, plus custody, nine dollars a week for the children, and three dollars a month for her "personal recreation." This final item, though minimal in amount, suggests that courts were willing to designate some money for amusements and consumption within the category of "necessities," which men were required to provide. Whatever other problems may be hidden from our view that contributed to this couple's woes, it is clear that money was a sore spot for a long time. Oscar's salary was hardly abundant, and he was finally unable to satisfy the demands of his wife and children to maintain their suburban lifestyle.[14]

Perhaps one of the most telling of these cases was the Los Angeles divorce of Margaret and Donald Wilton. She was a devout midwestern Protestant whose marriage to her clerk husband lasted two years. At one point she wrote to her estranged spouse, hoping to be reconciled. She recommended that he read some Bible passages relating to the duties of husbands and wives and promised to be a "good Christian wife." In a revealing statement at the end, she wrote,

I heard something about you that made my heart sing with joy; you have climbed another rung on the ladder of success. I am proud to know it, dear...

In spite of Donald's improved status, their marriage was beyond repair. After a rather bitter court battle, Margaret Wilton was granted a divorce.[15]

Families such as the ones mentioned above may not have suffered severe deprivation. But like other twentieth-century couples, they faced a greater potential for disappointment when a modicum of luxury became the anticipated norm. As the standard of living continued to climb, the golden age of affluence seemed imminent and was anticipated with almost religious fervor. For much of the American population, increasing prosperity apperared as a signal from the Divine that the culmination of progress was at hand. One observer perceived, "To most people a millenium implies spiritual overtones. So does the standard of living."[16] For a male provider, then, inability to keep up with this sanctified progress meant failure and damnation.

Although these pressures were particularly acute for the lower-middle class, they were also severe for workers. Financial difficulties among working-class couples, however, were qualitatively different from those facing white-collar families. They may not have felt the same status anxieties as petty proprietors or rank-and-file bureaucrats, but they lived with the uncertainties of a fluid labor market and usually lacked the cushion of corporate security. Weak or nonexistent labor unions left them fundamentally unprotected. This is not to deny that some of the abundance filtered down to the working classes. By 1900 their improved circumstances prompted Samuel Gompers, when asked if he thought the conditions of workers were worsening, to reply, "Oh, that is perfectly absurd."[17] Many low-income families in the 1920 period, however, still found it difficult to make ends meet. For these, luxuries were out of the question, and the affluence they saw everywhere around them only served to heighten frustrations.

Working-class couples, then, faced compounded difficulties. Often the breadwinner's earnings were inadequate and his job insecure. Moreover, he was subject to the same sorts of demands for mass-produced goods as his white-collar contemporaries. One significant feature of the consumer-oriented economy was the way it transcended class boundaries. On one level this contributed to a certain superficial "classless" quality. But on another level it served to homogenize tastes in a society where wealth remained unequally distributed. Once self-esteem and validation came to rest upon supplying material goods, those on the bottom rungs would be considered less worthy.

Alberta Raschke was a blue-collar wife in Los Angeles with a five-year-old daughter. She filed for a divoce on the grounds of desertion and neglect, claiming that her husband forced her to rely on her parents' charity. The couple married in Indiana in 1913, and separated four years later. At some point, Alberta came to California, and William remained in Chicago. In a letter, she accused him of refusing to support her and claimed that she was in a "weakened condition." "You have had ample time to *make a man of yourself* in all these six years, if you cared for your wife and baby, instead of driving a wagon for twelve dollars a week. You would not take work offered you at twenty-one dollars a week, so it is not because you could not find better. I stood for all the terrible abuse you gave me, and went without the very necessities of life to see if you would not come to your senses, but now I am tired of waiting and have decided to file suit for divorce.... I am as ever Alberta."[18]

Although Alberta Raschke probably had a valid complaint, the pressure put upon William to "make a man" of himself may have been unfair. It is not clear why he did not take the job allegedly offered to him for more pay, but perhaps he simply enjoyed what he was doing. The conflict between working at a job one liked and working for money may have ultimately led to this divorce. Perhaps William Raschke found the lower paying job more satisfying. But as far as his wife was concerned, the primary purpose of his work was to make money. Undoubtedly it was not easy for this woman to live on twelve dollars a week with a five-year-old child. Nevertheless, the equation of manhood with the ability to provide placed a particularly heavy burden on a laboring husband.

In general, working-class wives were less obsessed with status considerations and more concerned with bread-and-butter issues. Most blue-collar divorces that included money difficulties revolved around basic needs, similar to the conflicts that surfaced in the 1880s proceedings. These problems erupted frequently in New Jersey, where the majority of divorces were among blue-collar couples (see table 18). It is important to keep in mind that New Jersey only permitted divorces on the grounds of adultery and desertion—not financial neglect. Nevertheless, money was at the heart of many New Jersey litigations. In fact, a number of these couples struggled, quite literally, just to keep a roof over their heads.

A severe housing shortage in New Jersey's urban areas placed serious strains on several marriages. Providers with meager earnings often found themselves unable to provide a home. Numerous couples lived with parents or other relatives, or moved from one form of lodging to another. For these couples, the inability to acquire adequate housing was the fundamental issue that destroyed their marriages. The Shafers were one such family. "I want one thing," pleaded Anna Shafer to her husband. "Won't you please come back and make a home for me, I don't care if it is only two rooms, if you can afford to pay for two rooms." They had been married since 1910, when they ran away together to Hoboken, New Jersey. Anna claimed that William deserted her three years later. She said that her husband was "a drinking man who never made a home or provided for her and their child," although he worked for an insurance company. Anna was granted the divorce and restored to her maiden name.[19] The same problems ended the marriage of Harris and Catherine Martin, two blue-collar workers in Newark. "I told him I would go anyplace with him as long as he could furnish me with a home," explained Catherine. "I didn't care where it was, even if it was only one room and I was alone." But after three months they separated, and Catherine was granted a divorce plus the return of her maiden name.[20]

Lack of housing and insecure work also disrupted the marriage of a Jewish couple in New Jersey, Sarah and Morris Dubin, who married in 1910 and had one child that died. Morris was a tailor by trade but was unable to practice his craft. Instead he worked for the railroad, and as a cook in a sanitarium. It appears that this duo had a rather stormy marriage, with Morris deserting now and then and Sarah continually begging him to make a home for her. Whenever she asked, "Why won't you make me a home and support me?" he replied, "I won't and can't live in Newark with you." Newark was particularly plagued by the housing shortage at this time, which aggravated the situation for Morris, who was not able to find work that utilized his tailoring skills. But the court had little mercy. The interviewer concluded that Morris was "apparently one of those people who find it difficult to settle down and perform his obligations for any length of time." Sarah won her suit and the return of her maiden name.[21]

Although a chronic shortage of basic needs eroded most of these blue-collar marriages, a number of working-class couples quarreled over consumer spending and status concerns as well. A few cases illustrate how squabbles might ensue over how money should be spent. Emma Totsworth was nineteen when she married David Totsworth, a twenty-two-year-old machinist, in Jersey City. Five years later she deserted. When asked about their difficulties, David said they argued "over different things, like going out and clothes, no clean clothes and all around jealousy. Simple meanness. She spent money on clothes that should have gone for eating." It appears that David Totsworth preferred to see his hard-earned income used for less frivolous items.[22]

Charles and Ada Davis were plagued by similar problems. They were married in New Jersey in 1902 and had one child. After nine years, Ada deserted and went to New York. Apparently Charles, a railroad brakeman, never managed to provide for her in the style that she wanted. According to the interviewer, Ada became "dissatisfied with her surroundings and complained of the style of life her husband afforded her. She wouldn't speak or recognize her husband sometimes for days at a time. Finally she left, saying she wanted to live where she wanted to, and also wanted him to support her." Charles' brother stood up for the aggrieved husband, saying that he "always worked steadily and was a good provider for his home and did everything he could for his wife and family that a man could do under his circumstances." But apparently it was not enough. Charles testified that Ada "insisted upon telling me how much more the neighbors had than she had, and what the neighbor's husband did, and what they didn't do. I told her that if she would stop listening to outsiders and live for me and our little girl as she had done up to that time, everything could be very nice and we could get along." But Ada's dissatisfaction increased until she finally left, and Charles was granted a New Jersey divorce on the grounds of desertion.[23]

These blue-collar couples were plagued by status anxieties.

Both Emma Totsworth and Ada Davis had aspirations for material goods beyond the reach of their husbands' pay checks. Some wives not only held their spouses' incomes in disdain, they also looked down upon the work itself. Olivia Garside was a New Jersey housekeeper bent on feverish social climbing. After twenty-six years of marriage and three children, she finally left her husband Frederick, a machinist, who could not supply the lifestyle she craved. According to Frederick,

My wife never considered me her equal. She told me this shortly after our marriage, and she was never satisfied with anything I might undertake to do and that I was not as neat appearing as a professional man. She would say my conversation wasn't as it should be and she felt I was socially beneath her. I have always turned over every cent I made to my wife outside of my traveling expenses. I have never been intoxicated in my life. I would very often work overtime and on Sundays around the neighborhood to earn a few dollars more. My wife always complained I wasn't making enough money.

This husband took pride in his hard work, his efforts to support his wife, his sobriety and discipline. But to his wife, he lacked polish and grace—and the ample income to go with it. The court granted Frederick a divorce on the grounds of desertion.[24]

We have seen that providers faced a heavy burden in the early twentieth century. It was difficult enough for low-income families just to maintain a comfortable existence. In addition, blue-collar as well as white-collar husbands were expected to meet the material demands of a rising standard of living. Often this required stretching a modest budget to cover mass-produced luxury items as well as basic necessities. When desires rose to the point where a man was unable or unwilling to supply his wife's consumer aspirations, the marriage might fall apart. But this was not the end of it. Increasingly during these years, the provider's responsibility extended beyond the marriage itself. Often, men were obligated to support their wives indefinitely, through alimony, even after the marriage had legally come to an end.

Given the deeply rooted tradition that it was a husband's duty to provide for his wife, the legal provision for alimony appears logical. But if we look at the issue historically, this was not always the case. Originally, under common law, alimony was a concession to wives because husbands were entitled to keep dowries in case of divorce.[25] In America, however, the granting of alimony lost this equalizing function and took on new significance. Implicit in the provision for continued support is the notion that one tie might never be broken once the marriage has taken place: the duty of the husband to support his wife.

Ironically, during the very years of increasing opportunities for women to earn money for themselves, more wives were receiving alimony. Between 1900 and 1922, the proportion of American divorces granted with alimony nearly doubled.[26] This pattern is reflected in the Los Angeles samples. Among the 1880s group, 111 wives requested alimony, and only 44 were awarded support. In the 1920 sample, out of a total of 178 requests for alimony, 107 were awarded. This amounts to 32 percent of all divorces granted. The proportion of requests for continued support that were ultimately granted rose from 39 percent in the 1880s to 60 percent in 1920 (see table 20).

Although alimony was on the rise all over the country, some states were more likely to grant support than others. New Jersey courts, for example, were extremely reluctant to award alimony as late as 1920. Out of 218 divorces granted, only twelve included alimony. The California data, however, shows marked change over time. In the 1880s, alimony was relatively rare. As in New Jersey, there was no separate provision for child support, and awards appear to be geared to the needs of offspring. The data in table 21 show that a childless woman in the 1880s had almost no chance of getting alimony. Even in 1920, a Los Angeles mother was nearly three times as likely to be granted support as a divorcee without children. Yet the presence of children, while an important factor, was not the only condition for support, especially in the 1920 Los Angeles sample.

Neither the California nor the New Jersey laws specified under what circumstances alimony should be granted. We might expect the courts to provide support in cases where the husband earned a substantial salary. In all three samples, however, this consideration had little bearing on who actually requested and received alimony. As can be seen in table 22, in the 1880s, blue-collar husbands were just as likely to pay alimony as white-collar husbands; and in 1920 workers were only slightly less likely to pay alimony. In New Jersey, eight workers and only three white-collar husbands were required to pay alimony.

Much more startling, however, is the little difference it seemed to make if the woman worked as well. Ironically, the proportion of working wives granted alimony increased markedly during the very decades that it became easier for women to support themselves. In the earlier Los Angeles sample, only 4 percent of employed women were granted alimony. In the later Los Angeles sample, 44 percent of all wives who held jobs were awarded support (see table 23). Although many of the cases do not specify when the wife worked, the fact that these women had held jobs at some point indicates that they were capable of supporting themselves.

In the 1920 Los Angeles sample, women in all occupations were just as likely to request, and receive, alimony as nonworking wives. The smallest percentage of requests listed in table 24 came from professional women. This seems natural, for not only were professionals relatively well paid, but they probably gained a greater degree of satisfaction from their work and may have been content to continue working and supporting themselves. But it is worth noting that every professional woman who did request alimony was granted an award for support. Again, New Jersey in 1920 provides a sharp contrast. Only four of the alimony awards went to working wives (see table 23). Nevertheless, these four comprise one third of the alimony grants, which is a sizeable percentage. It should be noted, however, that all of these women had children in their custody.

What, then, were the criteria considered in granting alimony? In 1920 New Jersey, the primary issue appears to have been the presence of children. But in Los Angeles at the same time, the matter was not so simple. One consideration was who "won" the case. If the divorce was granted to the wife, it was much more likely that she would be granted alimony. In table 25 we see that in all three samples, very few of the cases won by husbands included alimony. No doubt women who filed for divorce were more likely to request alimony than those whose husbands filed against them. But this likelihood alone does not explain the discrepancy. A man's obligation to a woman he wronged was also involved. If the wife was granted the divorce, the husband was legally "guilty." Especially in the later period when alimony was more frequent, it may have been awarded as a kind of punishment.

In most cases, the amount of alimony granted was not large enough to allow wives to wallow in luxury (see table 26). Yet the issue appears in a different light when viewed from the husband's perspective, rather than according to the wife's needs. None of the men in the 1880s group claimed that their alimony payments were unfair. The issue was similarly non-controversial in the New Jersey sample. In the 1920 Los Angeles sample, however, several husbands felt that their wives' awards for support placed impossible burdens upon them.[27]

Robert Wheeler, for example, following his Los Angeles divorce from his wife Bertha, wrote bitterly that her "A-Lie–Money" would be late, due to his dental problems. He hoped that she would not "kick him while he's down." They were married in 1917, when he was a twenty-seven-year-old advertisement writer and she a seventeen-year-old clerk. Their marriage lasted about a year, during which time Robert held several jobs, including railroad work and employment in San Pedro shipyards. After bitter charges and counter-charges, Robert Wheeler was required to pay his young wife fifty dollars in fees and forty dollars out of his monthly one hundred dollar wages for a year. When times became difficult, the payments were nearly impossible to meet. After his first letter imploring her not to cause him legal problems, he wrote again, more desperately. He threatened to expose her for adultery, put the story in the papers, and send it to all her relatives in the South. She could avoid this embarrassment by giving him a receipt for $550—all the alimony and fees due her. If she refused, he assured her that he would make her ashamed to show her face in public, concluding, "You can expect no mercy from me." Robert seems nasty in these letters; but he found himself cornered into an obligation that could not fulfill. It was especially painful considering there were no children, and he was forced to support a healthy young working woman, merely because they had been married for a brief time. He felt his payments not only impossible, but unreasonable. His threats, however, backfired; he ended up in jail for five days.[28]

Although alimony was often awarded without considering the husband's income, the amount might be specified according to his ability to pay. Occasionally, payments were adjusted after the divorce with alterations in the status of either spouse. In cases where the amount was increased, it was usually due to the needs of the children or changes in the wife's situation. But adjustments might also reflect the husband's good fortune, increasing his payments regardless of the woman's needs. This is an important point, for it implies that a woman was entitled to share in the upward mobility of her former spouse, even though she was no longer married to him. On the other hand, as in the case of Robert Wheeler cited above, if the man's resources declined, his obligation was not necessarily diminished accordingly.

One case of this nature involved a well-known film actor and director, Erich Von Stroheim. He was married to his first wife in 1918; at the time they had a two-year-old son. After five months of married life, they separated. Soon after, his wife, May, sued for divorce on the grounds of extreme cruelty, saying that her husband

loafed around the house and failed to secure any employment. . . . When he finally secured employment he squandered his money on other women and neglected his wife. . . . When earning $150 a week for Universal Films he refused to give her any money for her or their child, and spent it all in the company of other women.

She asked for court fees, custody, and fifty dollars a month alimony. In reply, the director asserted that his wife was earning "large sums in regular and continuous employment" and did not need any contribution from him toward her support. He claimed that she earned seventy-five dollars a week as a costume designer and a "high salaried motion picture actress." The court, however, granted her the divorce, custody of their child, and fifteen dollars a week.

But the case did not end there. In 1922, May claimed that since the film maker now earned two thousand dollars a week she should have her award increased from fifteen dollars to seventy-five dollars per week. The court granted her request. Two years later, Stroheim requested a reduction in payments, since his income the previous year was less than one-third of his anticipated $110,000. The request was denied. The pro-

ceedings continued until 1940, with the wife constantly attempting to adjust her allotment according to his soaring
career, and the wealthy director resisting every change. He
argued that he had remarried, and had a small child, plus a
mother and crippled brother to support. The court had little
sympathy for his difficulties and fined him for contempt. The
battles continued until his son reached maturity in 1940 and
signed an agreement stating that his father had fulfilled all
obligations.[29] Obviously, in this case Stroheim was not forced
to pay beyond his means. He was quite wealthy and fully capable of maintainting his first wife and child in comfort, if not
luxury. But the principle underlying the continued adjustments
is significant. The amount of support was determined according to the husband's financial status, even years after the divorce.

The divorce data indicate that in spite of increasing opportunities for women to work, divorcing wives in 1920 appeared
hardly more enthusiastic about supporting themselves than
their earlier counterparts, with a few striking exceptions.
Moreover, many wives expected their husbands to supply the
necessities of "lifestyle" as well as "life." This was not due to
any inherent lack of eagerness on the part of women; rather, it
was a direct result of the lack of viable options elsewhere. If a
woman did enter the work force, it was on men's terms. But at
home, she could determine her own hours of work and choose
her own routine, which was more flexible, if not more interesting, than most available jobs. Most of all, perhaps, she
could be her own boss—something increasingly difficult even
for men, but almost impossible for women in the work world.
As remuneration, she had access to her husband's pay check,
which was more than she was likely to be able to earn on her
own. In terms of convenience, satisfaction, and monetary rewards, most of the women in the divorce samples seemed to
prefer the role of dependent housewife. In this sense, the
statements and experiences of these divorcing wives serve as
bitter testimony to the failure of modern economic and political
institutions to effect meaningful changes in the quality of life
for the average American woman. As long as the economic
system offered women satisfaction as consumers and frustration as producers, women would continue to look to the home
for fulfillment and to men for support.

Epilogue:
The Pursuit of Happiness

Mercy and justice to the mismated are creeping into the law. Without doubt marriage is throwing off the shackles of blind intolerance and groping toward a form in which human beings may find sanity and contentment. . . . Divorce—like medical anesthesia—so lately despised, is beginning to be recognized as the next great step along the way. The way to where? The only answer is happiness.[1]

The pursuit of happiness took on a new direction and urgency in the decades surrounding the turn of the century. Focusing on private life, men and women turned to each other and to the home in a fervent personal quest, dramatically reflected in the rising rate of marriage and the soaring rate of divorce. The hundreds of court cases used in this study provide a rare glimpse into marriage and family life during the years when marital breakdown rose most rapidly, revealing the thoughts and emotions of ordinary individuals facing a major crisis in their lives. Taken together, they reflect a larger historical drama: the emergence of modern American life and the great expectations for personal fulfillment that came with it.

The story unfolds in the 1880s, in a growing city on the western edge of the American frontier. Here we find the heirs of Victorianism forging a new community and establishing religious, political, and cultural institutions. As they took hold of the reins of power, they began the task of building a city in tune with their cultural ideals. The divorce cases filed during this decade indicate the strength of the Victorian world view these settlers brought with them. Compared to later decades, divorce was relatively rare. When it did occur, it was usually among these native Americans themselves, whose marriages did not meet traditional standards. If one spouse flagrantly violated the code of behavior expected within marriage, the

other would seek a divorce. We find very little confusion, ambivalence, or contention over these accepted roles.

Women discarded husbands if they failed in the fundamental
duty of providing the necessities of life: a comfortable place to
live, enough to eat, and adequate means for reasonable well
being. If they polluted the domestic environment through
overindulgence in vices such as drinking or gambling, they
were deemed unworthy. Sexual excess was also beyond the
bounds of reasonable behavior. The limits and duties were
clearly defined: husbands were to provide the necessities of
life, treat their wives with courtesy and protection, and exercise sexual restraint. Men who found that their wives deviated
from proper norms of conduct also sought redress. A wife's
duty was to maintain a comfortable home, take care of household chores, bear and tend to the children, and set the moral
tone for domestic life. She was to remain chaste and modest in
her behavior, frugal in matters of household expenses, and her
conduct was never to reflect badly upon her home and her
husband's good name. A woman who was not genteel in her
demeanor, who acted like (or indeed was) a "whore," or who
violated the boundaries—physical as well as moral—of a
woman's proper sphere, might be shed in the divorce court.
The roles for both husbands and wives, then, were well under-
stood. These norms formed the basic requirements for attain-
ing domestic peace and building solid communities around
well-disciplined homes.

As couples whose marriages did not conform to these standards headed for divorce, the vast majority of their contemporaries stayed married and went about the task of building
a city that would provide an appropriate setting for their moral
homes. They closed vice districts, outlawed prostitution,
raised the age of consent, established churches, closed saloons
on Sundays, and set up supervised recreational facilities. Yet
these efforts were not aimed toward preserving the past; the
goal was to build a better future. Ennui had crept into work and
public life. Americans were restless and reaching out for new
experiences. Faced with the decline of Victorian traditions,
they tried to shape their environment in a way that would allow
the positive aspects of modern life to flourish, while screening
out the negative elements. As a part of this effort they built
sprawling suburban homes in protected neighborhoods and

created legitimate amusements which would provide constructive and wholesome recreation. As they accumulated more money and more free time in which to spend it, these migrants to Los Angeles, like their contemporaries all over the country, sought to make affluence and leisure both safe and satisfying. In this pursuit, they turned with increased fervor to the private side of life, perhaps to compensate for a loss of satisfactions elsewhere.

What, then, did these modern urbanites want out of marriage by 1920? Had they buried the remnants of Victorianism, in the quest for a life truly liberated from the past? This study suggests that such was not the case. Men and women in 1920 seemed to want a more satisfying home. But there was a confusion surrounding domestic aspirations that had not been present in the 1880s. "Marital happiness" was not clearly defined; no universal standard held for everyone. Contrary to the assumptions of contemporary observers as well as historians since, most divorcing urbanites were not in the vanguard of a moral revolution. Although they displayed desires for new excitement and sensuality, most were caught between traditions of the past and visions of the future.

In general, wives in 1920 still preferred care and protection to a job and independence. Like their grandmothers, they wanted husbands to provide for them and respect their delicacy. These modern women were still antagonistic to sexual excesses and inclined toward a peaceful domestic life with children, albeit with greater opportunities for fun, leisure, and affluence than their Victorian predecessors. Men in the sample reflected similar ambivalence. They may have been attracted to youthful and exciting "new women," but they also wanted domestic, frugal, and virtuous wives who would keep house and tend to the children. These expectations held true for couples in New Jersey as well as Los Angeles, with very few variations. There is no reason to assume that significant differences appeared anywhere else in the country.

If most moral attitudes survived the early decades of the twentieth century without radical changes, this is not to imply that aspirations surrounding marriage and family life had not altered. Traditional notions of virtue were enveloped by modern desires, heightening hopes for marital fulfillment. This overlapping of cultural values caused a great deal of upheaval in many marriages, as a number of the cases in this study suggest. Divorces often resulted from a myriad of problems, rather than one specific issue. The case mentioned at the very beginning of this study illustrates how numerous difficulties might erupt simultaneously. Lorimer Linganfield was attracted to a sensual, exciting young woman, but was chagrined when she refused to settle down into proper wifely behavior. His wife, in turn, was excited by the new life, especially urban amusements, and wanted a man who would provide high-level affluence. Unlike most of her contemporaries, she did not want children. But similar to many Victorians, she was reluctant to have sex with her husband, in spite of her sexy appearance.[2]

The pursuit of happiness took couples like the Linganfields into wedlock, and then out again. Along with marriage, divorce was another step in the quest. But the break itself was rarely a happy one. In fact, it was almost always painful. Rather than a triumph, it often seemed like a personal failure. In the divorce court, unhappily married individuals blamed their spouses. But away from the court, they often blamed themselves. The cases in this study are filled with highly emotional expressions of remorse. As one errant husband wrote to his wife:

As a man, I should have acted differently, but through all these years my whole system has been poisoned with drink. . . . Your struggle, working and saving, was the only way . . . but I, like a fool, couldn't realize that. . . . I don't believe any other woman would have put up with as much as you have. You were a neat, good housekeeper who lived for and loved a good home. But already I am suffering from remorse. . . . I often wish myself dead in order to have an end to it all. . . . We will go our separate ways—good bye from Adolph.[3]

Similar was the statement of Henry Northam, a piano salesman and tuner, married to Elizabeth, an "even tempered, church going" woman who "worked until she had a breakdown." They lived together for seven years after their marriage in 1905 and had no children. When the case for desertion had been granted, Henry wrote his wife a letter, saying he was not resentful. He claimed that his "illness" had been the "sole cause of our disaster. . . . I was a victim of ignorance and superstition and the penalty is unavoidable." Yet he will cherish what had been "ideal" between them and hopes that she will find someone and make a "happy home for which you are rarely and richly endowed by nature."[4] Another such case was that of Harrison Drinon, whose wife Mary divorced him on the grounds of habitual intemperance. After a twenty-five-year marriage beginning in Illinois in 1882, he wrote,

I am quite well aware that my actions of late precluded the possibility of my returning to the house and very deservedly so....I seek no sympathy, for I deserve it all. I have been a failure as a husband and father and in every other conceivable way.[5]

Perhaps the most moving and poignant of these cases of remorse is of a woman who defied the very essence of virtue: chastity and marital fidelity. Yet in her misery she indicated what had led to her downfall. Rose and Charles Pearson were married in Cameron, Missouri, in 1910. Their union came to an end when Charles discovered a letter from his wife's lover, a married man who urged that they both divorce and marry each other. Rose's anguished response overflowed with guilt—and yet this ultimate violation of marital vows did not represent any flaunting of wedlock or any rejection of the domestic ideal. In fact, it was the very pursuit of that personalized relationship that led to her adultery:

I am blind and stunned.... My suffering and sin is greater than I can bear. I deserve all.... Will try to answer questions while I am able to write. The date of first sin was the last day of October. Never on bed, I held that sacred. No, no, not daily, and altogether five times.... I never had any of my clothes off not even my corset. Always dressed. He gave me altogether $75. I fought till I could fight no longer.... He promised me a home a future and a little one . . .

Here Rose revealed her own marital disappointments, and the promise of fulfillment with her lover. It was not illicit excitement she sought; rather, it was a "home a future and a little one," desires not satisfied by her husband. Yet even in the midst of sexual relations with another man, she did not transgress easily. Indeed, she still held her marriage bed "sacred." Her confession, however, contained several accusations: lack of spending money which her lover apparently supplied, security with the promise of children, and an affectionate man at her side. Communication with her husband broke down, and Rose found solace with another.

I do not ask you to take me back, I hoped and prayed you
would take me into your arms again. Now I have lost last.
There is only one thing left. Death. One last favor I ask of
you dear Charles do not tell my sisters all my sin and
wrong.... It is torture for me to stay here under this
sin.... Charles, I know there were times when I did not speak
to you. I needed your love then, that was all that was the
matter. I was aching and hungry for love. One loving word
then or if you had taken me in your arms would have made
me happy again ... and that would have drawn us closer together. You never could understand this and you left me
alone to suffer in silence.

Rose was left with her wish to die rather than face her shame.
The home she so desired now seemed beyond her grasp. Yet
she blamed her husband for his lack of responsiveness and
reproached him for being totally oblivious to her needs. This
woman did not want independence. Her marriage ended because of her unfulfilled desires for affection, security and
domesticity. Her husband remained detached, unable to comprehend:

When I needed your love most you withheld it. Forgive
me my husband. Forgive me is the cry in my heart.... Pray
for me my husband and if you hear of my death in the next
few weeks or month you will know what to say to shield my
name from public shame.... I have loved you more than I
realized.... I am heartbroken, helpless, and alone and
forsaken. My husband, try to forgive, the girl you never
seemed to understand what she wanted—*much love*.
Your lost Rose.[6]

Rose Pearson felt lost. She failed in her primary role in life.
Like many of her contemporaries, her quest for happiness led
her away from her disappointing marriage toward the promise
of a better one. The desperation of these wives reflects the high
stakes placed on marriage. Because most women viewed matrimony as the only place they could truly express themselves,
it is misleading to equate the desire for marital dissolution with
any widespread urge for freedom from marriage itself. The
high rate of remarriage among divorced persons testifies to this
fact. Those who divorced once often divorced twice, as our
Los Angeles sample from 1920 illustrates (see table 27).
Twenty-six of the women and eleven of the men had been
divorced at least once prior to the filing of this action. Out of

those whose marital status was known, this represents 18 percent of the women and 8 percent of the men. It is significant that over twice as many women as men were headed for their second divorce, in spite of their younger age. These findings suggest that divorce did not indicate a rejection of marriage; rather, it reflected the increased personal desires that matrimony was expected to satisfy, especially for women.

Although men who sued for divorce were just as likely as women to have petitions granted in their favor, most of the cases were filed by wives (see table 28). More eager for domestic perfection, women were also more easily disappointed. Realizing this, one judge admonished a dissatisfied young wife without concealing his exasperation. He felt that her hopes for happiness were unrealistically high:

I think it is another of the cases in which the husband did not treat his wife as he should and she was in a pretty big hurry to get a divorce. So she puts together everything that happened in their domestic history to make out extreme cruelty. . . . I do not understand why she is in such a hurry. . . . She will probably get married again and have some more trouble. . . . It is not going to hurt this young woman at all not to have a decree of divorce just now. This is the judgment. . . . She is hereby denied a decree of divorce.[7]

This judge, no doubt, had heard more than one too many pleas for divorce; his attitude was undeniably callous. Yet he perceived a profound reality: marriage was not likely to sustain the high hopes that all too often were brought to it. When these hopes were shattered, the result was tragedy rather than triumph. One Los Angeles divorcee wanted to let the presiding judge know that her successful decree was purchased at the cost of tremendous emotional suffering:

I hardly presume you have much personal interest in cases tried before you, but I do want to say a little bit about the case just finished, and to thank you for the decision; and yet, your Honor, that decision did not cause the heart thrill you seemed to anticipate, for I loved my husband up to the time of his desertion, which was a staggering blow to me. . . . Anyway, I am placed in the position of having to thank you for making of me something I never wanted to be—a divorced woman. Very respectfully, Mayme E. Johnson.[8]

Divorce represents a painful step on the road to personal fulfillment. Scenes of marital failure, admittedly, are not the place to look for happiness. Obviously, broken marriages cannot serve as examples of marriages in general. But were the couples in the divorce samples really deviations from the norm, or were they rather the "tip of the iceberg," representing only a fraction of couples with similar problems who managed to live with their difficulties? I suspect that the problems we have explored here were not unique to failing marriages, but existed to a greater or lesser degree among far more couples than ever reached the divorce court.[9] Indeed, as the twentieth century has progressed, we have seen more and more of the iceberg. Americans are still coupling, uncoupling, and recoupling at an astonishing rate.[10]

Today, broken marriage has lost the stigma it had a century ago. Divorced persons are no longer considered social mishaps or moral deviants. But is divorce really a liberation? Do people discard matrimony in favor of other alternatives—or do they merely move on in a perpetual quest for "the perfect relationship"? Personal life seems to have become a national obsession in 20th century America. It is not likely that the domestic domain will ever be able to satisfy completely the great expectations for individual fulfillment brought to it. As long as the American pursuit of happiness continues along this private path, divorce is likely to be with us.

Appendix: Tables

165

TABLE 1 Marriage and Divorce Rates: United States, 1870–1950

	Marriages per 1,000 eligibles[a]	Divorces per 1,000 marriages
1870	8.8	1.5
1880	9.0	2.2
1890	9.0	3.0
1900	9.3	4.0
1910	10.3	4.5
1920	12.0	7.7
1930	9.2	7.4
1940	12.1	8.7
1950	11.0	10.2

SOURCE: Paul H. Jacobson, *American Marriage and Divorce* (New York, 1959), pp. 21, 90.
[a]Standardized for age and sex ratios.

TABLE 2 Median Age at First Marriage, by Sex: United States, 1890–1930

	Men	Women
1890	26.1	22.0
1900	25.9	21.9
1910	25.1	21.6
1920	24.6	21.2
1930	24.3	21.3

SOURCE: U. S. Bureau of Commerce, *Historical Statistics of the United States* (Washington D.C., 1975), p. 19.

TABLE 3 Nativity and Racial Composition of Divorce Samples and Los Angeles Populations, 1880–90 and 1920 (Percentages)

	L.A. Population, 1890[a]	Litigants, 1880s Sample	L.A. Population, 1920	Litigants, 1920 Sample
	(N=50,395)	(N=1,000)	(N=576,673)	(N=1,000)
Native white	72	79	76	78
Foreign-born white	21	13	14	10
"Colored"[b]	7	—	—	—
Asian	—	—	3	2
Spanish-surnamed	—	8	4	6
Negro	—	—	3	4

SOURCES: U.S. Bureau of the Census, *Eleventh Census of the United States, 1890; Fourteenth Census of the United States, 1920;* and data gathered from the divorce samples.
[a] The 1890 census was the first to include a breakdown of the Los Angeles population.
[b] In the 1890 census, all Negroes, Chinese, Japanese, and American Indians were included under the "Colored" category.

TABLE 4 Nativity and Racial Composition of Divorce Samples and Married Control Groups, L.A., 1880s and 1920 (Percentages)

	1880s		1920	
	Divorce	Control	Divorce	Control
	(N=1000)	(N=257)	(N=1,000)	(N=212)
Native white	79	60	78	75
Foreign-born white	13	16	10	14
Black	1	0	4	7
Spanish-surnamed	6	21	6	2
Other	1	3	2	2

SOURCES: Data collected from divorce samples plus control statistics gathered from marriage licenses filed in Los Angeles. The marriage license dates were chosen to correspond with the years in which couples in the divorce samples married.

TABLE 5 Birthplace of Native Americans and Foreign-Born in Los Angeles Population, Control Groups, and Divorce Samples, 1880s and 1920 (Percentages)

Native Americans

| | 1880s | | | | 1920 | | | | |
| | Control | | Divorce | | L.A. | Control | | Divorce | |
	Husbands	Wives	Husbands	Wives	Population	Husbands	Wives	Husbands	Wives
	(N=81)	(N=91)	(N=86)	(N=111)	(N=434,807)	(N=80)	(N=86)	(N=151)	(N=147)
New England	7	2	14	14	4	1	4	3	2
Middle Atlantic	20	8	13	13	11	10	9	14	14
East North Central	17	20	21	22	23	18	25	29	26
West North Central	17	16	11	10	17	22	22	19	19
South Atlantic	5	3	7	8	3	5	5	2	2
East South Central	4	3	10	10	4	10	7	5	5
West South Central	9	6	4	4	5	5	5	7	10
Mountain	0	2	1	1	6	7	7	8	8
Pacific	21	40	19	18	27	22	16	13	14

Foreign-Born

| | 1880s | | | | 1920 | | | | |
| | Control | | Divorce | | L.A. | Control | | Divorce | |
	Husbands	Wives	Husbands	Wives	Population	Husbands	Wives	Husbands	Wives
	(N=39)	(N=26)	(N=44)	(N=16)	(N=115,334)	(N=25)	(N=19)	(N=32)	(N=34)
Great Britain	28	11	23	50	25	12	16	16	38
Ireland	3	4	7	12	5	4	16	0	3
Scandinavia, Germany, Austria	23	27	32	20	9	32	21	9	6
Western Europe	—	—	—	—	15	—	—	12	6
Eastern Europe	—	—	—	—	16	16	16	23	22
Southern Europe	20	15	23	12	9	20	16	25	16
Latin America, including Mexico	23	39	10	6	20	8	10	9	6
Orient, other	3	4	5	—	1	8	5	6	3

NOTE: The 1880 census did not provide a breakdown of the Los Angeles population.

TABLE 6 Working Women in Divorce Samples and in Adult Female Populations

	Number of Employed Wives in Sample	Proportion of Total Women in Sample	Number of Employed Women in Total Population	Proportion of Total Adult Female Population
Los Angeles, 1880s	167	33%	3,412	23%
Los Angeles, 1920	206	41%	68,400	28%
New Jersey, 1920	95	42%	295,990	24%

SOURCES: Divorce proceedings, city directories, and census figures.

TABLE 7 Working Wives' Complaints about Work and Support

	L.A., 1880s	L.A., 1920	N.J., 1920
Husband "neglects to provide"	122	90	84
Wife forced to work against her wishes	30	37	63
Miscellaneous complaints of neglect	14	20	6
Wife indicates a desire to work	0	9	5
Total working wives	167	206	95

NOTE: Total number of complaints may exceed total number of working wives, since several women made more than one of the above comments. This was especially true in New Jersey, where the litigants were interviewed. Most of the New Jersey wives who complained about having to work also claimed that their husbands neglected to provide for them.

TABLE 8 Occupations of Husbands and Wives in Los Angeles Divorce Sample, 1880s; Men and Women in Los Angeles Work Force, 1890

	Husbands		Male Work Force		Wives		Female Work Force	
	Number	Percentage	Number	Percentage	Number	Percentage	Number	Percentage
High white collar								
Professional	23	7	958	6	5	7	468	14
Major proprietor	40	13	837	5	1	1	—	—
Subtotal	63	20	1,795	11	6	8	468	14
Low White Collar								
Clerks, sales	24	8	2,369	15	0	—	315	9
Semiprofessional	2	>1	169	1	3	4	188	6
Petty proprietor	86	28	2,643	17	18	25	192	6
Subtotal	112	36	5,181	33	21	29	695	21
High blue collar								
Skilled worker	71	23	3,095	20	15	21	781	23
Low blue collar								
Semiskilled worker	28	9	2,545	16	4	5	110	3
Unskilled worker	37	12	3,051	20	27	37	1,358	39
Subtotal	65	21	5,596	36	31	42	1,468	41
Total	311	100	15,667	100	73	100	3,412	100

SOURCES: Divorce proceedings, city directories, and census figures.
NOTE: Totals refer to occupations that were specified; unspecified occupations were deleted. Nearly every man worked, but only 311 indicated specific jobs. Of the women litigants, 167 held jobs, but only 73 were identified.

TABLE 9 Moral Complaints Mentioned by Litigants

	Complaints by Husbands			Complaints by Wives		
	L.A., 1880s	L.A., 1920	N.J., 1920	L.A., 1880s	L.A., 1920	N.J., 1920
Drinking	11	3	5	52	19	12
Gambling	0	1	3	1	5	4
Drug addiction	3	2	1	1	0	1
Night life	1	16	12	2	8	5
Being called "whore"	—	—	—	23	19	7
Laziness, neglect of chores	18	13	9	—	—	—
Failure to be "ladylike"	16	4	2	—	—	—

TABLE 10 Median Age at Marriage

	Men	Women
United States general population[a]		
1890	26.1	22.0
1900	25.9	21.9
1910	25.1	21.6
1920	24.6	21.2
1930	24.3	21.3
Los Angeles litigants		
1880s[b]	29.2	20.6
1920[a]	24.0	19.7
New Jersey litigants		
1920[b]	29.2	17.2

SOURCES: U.S. Bureau of the Census, *Historical Statistics of the United States* (Washington, D.C., 1960); and divorce proceedings.
[a] Age at first marriage
[b] Sample includes several people married for the second or third time.

TABLE 11 Disposition of Children: Requests and Settlements

	Requests			Settlements		
	L.A., 1880s	L.A., 1920	N.J., 1920	L.A., 1880s	L.A., 1920	N.J., 1920
Custody for the wife	161	133	49	129	76	31
Custody for the husband	24	27	22	20	12	12
Custody for a third party	3	3	1	2	1	1
Children divided	8	1	0	15	1	0

NOTE: It is interesting that in the 1880s sample, children were more likely to be placed in the custody of the husband, or divided, than in the later samples. This is probably because children legally "belonged" to fathers during most of the nineteenth century. In all three divorce samples, however, the vast majority of dispositions gave custody to the mother.

TABLE 12 Number of Children Reported by Couples

	Couples in Sample					
		1880s		1920		1920
Number of Children	L.A., Number	Per-centage	L.A., Number	Per-centage	N.J., Number	Per-centage
0	210	45	238	48	90	41
1	81	17	117	23	66	30
2	74	16	58	12	27	12
3	44	9	18	4	11	5
4	21	5	11	2	3	1
5	13	3	1	>1	2	1
6	2	>1	3	>1	4	2
Over 6	5	1	0	0	2	1
Children of previous marriage	9	2	25	5	8	4
Adult children	5	1	19	4	3	1
Unknown	2	>1	10	2	5	2

TABLE 13 Complaints Involving Children

	Complaints by Husbands			Complaints by Wives		
	L.A., 1880s	L.A., 1920	N.J., 1920	L.A., 1880s	L.A., 1920	N.J., 1920
Cruelty to children	4	4	2	12	13	6
Neglect of child-care responsibilities	4	12	4	0	0	0
Corruption of children	2	2	0	1	6	0
Influencing of children against spouse	2	6	1	11	7	5
Spouse's not wanting to have children	0	4	0	0	6	2
Abortion against husband's will	2	2	0	0	0	0
Husband's demanding or forcing an abortion	0	0	0	0	5	1

TABLE 14 Sexual Complaints of Litigants

	L.A., 1880s	L.A., 1920	N.J., 1920
Complaints by husbands			
Sexual abuse	0	0	0
Spouse too demanding	1	5	2
Refusal to have sex	10	12	6
Venereal disease	0	3	1
Premarital sex	3	4	10
Total	14	24	19
Complaints by wives			
Sexual abuse	6	16	9
Spouse too demanding	0	10	7
Refusal to have sex/impotence	2	11	2
Venereal disease	1	8	1
Premarital sex	0	0	0
Total	9	45	19

Table 15 Legal Grounds for Divorce and Annulment

	L.A., 1880s		L.A., 1920		N.J., 1920[a]	
	Number	Percentage	Number	Percentage	Number	Percentage
Desertion	181	39	219	46	141	64
Extreme cruelty	166	35	138	29	—	—
Adultery	43	9	32	7	75	34
Neglect	47	10	51	11	—	—
Intemperance	26	6	16	3	—	—
Felony conviction	3	>1	3	>1	—	—
Valid previous marriage[b]	2	>1	13	3	—	—
Fraud, coercion[b]	0	0	5	>1	5	2

NOTE: This table includes only the primary legal ground upon which the petition was originally filed. Other complaints were often included in the proceedings, and are included in tabulations elsewhere (see, for instance, table 9) as well as in the text.
[a] Only two grounds for divorce were legal in New Jersey in 1920. The last category indicates annulment petitions.
[b] Grounds for annulment.

Table 16 Sexual Complaints by Occupational Category

	L.A., 1880s		L.A., 1920		N.J., 1920	
	Sexual Abuse/ Too Demanding Spouse	Rufusal/ Incapacity	Sexual Abuse/ Too Demanding Spouse	Refusal/ Incapacity	Sexual Abuse/ Too Demanding Spouse	Refusal/ Incapacity
White collar						
Husbands	1	4	2	6	1	3
Wives	3	1	10	5	5	1
Blue collar						
Husbands	0	6	3	6	1	3
Wives	2	1	13	6	7	1

NOTE: Occupations were not stated in every case. The above figures include only those cases where both sexual problems and occupational category were given.

TABLE 17 Occupations of Husbands and Wives in Los Angeles 1920 Divorce
Sample; and Men and Women in Los Angeles Work Force, 1920

	Husbands		Male Work Force	Wives		Female Work Force
	Number	Percentage	Percentage	Number	Percentage	Percentage
High white collar						
Professional	13	4	6	13	8	8
Major proprietor	15	4	4	1	>1	1
Subtotal	*28*	*8*	*10*	*14*	*8*	*9*
Low white collar						
Clerk, sales	59	16	20	62	36	33
Semiprofessional	15	4	3	13	8	8
Petty proprietor	48	13	4	12	7	2
Subtotal	*122*	*33*	*27*	*87*	*51*	*43*
High blue collar						
Skilled foreman	95	26	32	10	6	7
Low blue collar						
Semiskilled						
worker	99	28	6	32	18	9
Unskilled worker	14	4	25	30	17	32
Subtotal	*113*	*32*	*31*	*62*	*35*	*41*
Total	358	100%	197,700	173	100%	68,400

SOURCES: Divorce proceedings, city directories, and census figures.
NOTE: Three hundred fifty eight of the husbands indicated specific jobs; 173 of
the 206 employed women indicated specific occupations.

TABLE 18 Occupations of Litigants (N. J. 1920)

	Husbands		Wives	
	Number	Percentage	Number	Percentage
High white collar				
Professional	8	4	5	6
Major proprietor	9	5	1	1
Subtotal	*17*	*9*	*6*	*7*
Low white collar				
Clerk, sales	30	16	25	26
Semiprofessional	7	4	3	3
Petty proprietor	16	9	2	2
Subtotal	*53*	*29*	*30*	*31*
High blue collar				
Skilled foreman	40	22	10	11
Low blue collar				
Semiskilled worker	39	21	25	26
Unskilled worker	34	19	24	25
Subtotal	*73*	*40*	*49*	*51*
Total	183	100	95	100

NOTE: As the divorce statistics are from localities throughout the state, there is no available breakdown of the New Jersey state labor force for comparison.

TABLE 19 Total Number of Financial Conflicts Appearing in Proceedings, by Husband's Occupational Level

	L.A., 1880s	L.A., 1920	N.J., 1920
Upper white collar	10	8	4
Lower white collar	26	54	25
Blue collar	43	39	32

NOTE: For total number of litigants in each occupational category, see tables 8, 17 and 18.

TABLE 20 Alimony Requests and Awards

	L.A., 1880s		L.A., 1920		N.J., 1920	
	Number	Percentage	Number	Percentage	Number	Percentage
Requests	111		178		39	
Wives requesting alimony		22		36		17
Number of awards	44		107		12	
Wives receiving awards		9		21		5
Requests receiving awards		40		60		31

TABLE 21 Alimony Granted According to Presence of Children

	L.A., 1880s			L.A., 1920			N.J., 1920		
	Number of Cases	Number Granted Alimony	Percentage Granted Alimony	Number of Cases	Number Granted Alimony	Percentage Granted Alimony	Number of Cases	Number Granted Alimony	Percentage Granted Alimony
Children present	240	32	13	223	77	35	115	10	9
No children present	226	8	3	258	34	13	90	2	2

TABLE 22 Alimony Granted According to Husband's Occupation

	L.A., 1880s[a]		L.A., 1920[b]		N.J., 1920[c]	
	Percentage of Husbands in Sample	Percentage of Alimony Awards	Percentage of Husbands in Sample	Percentage of Alimony Awards	Percentage of Husbands in Sample	Percentage of Alimony Awards
White collar						
Upper	20	23	8	8	11	0
Lower	36	33	35	43	29	33
Subtotal	*56*	*56*	*43*	*51*	*40*	*33*
Blue collar						
Upper	23	29	26	18	21	47
Lower	21	15	31	31	39	20
Subtotal	*44*	*44*	*57*	*49*	*60*	*67*

[a] Total awards = 44.
[b] Total awards = 107.
[c] Total awards = 12.

TABLE 23 Alimony Granted According to Working Status of Wives

	L.A., 1880s	L.A., 1920	N.J., 1920
Number of working wives	167	206	95
Number of working wives granted alimony	7	91	4
Percentage of working wives granted alimony	4	44	4

TABLE 24 Alimony Requests and Awards According to Occupation of Wives (L.A., 1920)

	Number of Wives	Number of Wives Requesting Alimony	Percentage of Wives Requesting Alimony	Number of Wives Granted Alimony	Percentage of Requests Awarded
Professional	13	2	15	2	100
Major proprietor	1	1	100	0	0
Clerks	62	24	39	18	75
Semiprofessional	13	4	31	2	50
Petty proprietor	12	3	25	3	100
Skilled	10	4	40	2	50
Semiskilled	32	12	38	8	75
Unskilled	30	8	27	6	75

NOTE: Owing to the small number of working wives granted alimony in the Los Angeles 1880s sample and the 1920 New Jersey sample (see table 23), a comparable occupational breakdown was not possible.

TABLE 25 Alimony Granted According to Which Spouse Was Granted Divorce

	L.A., 1880s		L.A., 1920		N.J., 1920	
	To husband	To wife	To husband	To wife	To husband	To wife
Divorces granted	105	266	104	233	95	123
Divorces granted with alimony	5	39	10	97	4	8

TABLE 26 Alimony Awards per Month

	L.A., 1880s	L.A., 1920	N.J., 1920
$10–50	15	75	9
$60–100	4	21	—
$100–200	—	6	—
Over $200	—	3	—
Cases with specific dollar amount	19	105	9
Cases with amount unspecified	25	2	3

TABLE 27 Previous Marital Status of Husbands and Wives at Time of Marriage
(L.A., 1920)

	Number of Husbands	Percentage of Husbands of Known Status	Number of Wives	Percentage of Wives of Known Status
Divorced once	11	8	26	18
Divorced twice	1	>1	0	0
Windowed once	13	9	11	8
Widowed twice	1	>1	1	>1
Previously married (present status unknown)	2	1	3	2
Single	118	81	105	72

TABLE 28 Parties Filing Action and Disposition of Cases (L.A., 1920)

	Action Filed by	Decree Granted to	Percentage Granted Decrees
Wife	350	233	67
Husband	149	104	70

Notes

INTRODUCTION

1. Case D492, 1920, Los Angeles County Archives. All subsequent cases from Los Angeles are located in the Los Angeles County Archives. Those from New Jersey are in the New Jersey State Records in Trenton, New Jersey. Names have been modified to protect the privacy of the individuals and their families.

2. Alfred Cahen, *Statistical Analysis of American Divorce* (New York, 1932), pp. 15, 21.

3. Walter F. Willcox, *The Divorce Problem* (New York, 1897), pp. 66–67.

4. James P. Lichtenberger, *Divorce, A Study in Social Causation* (New York, 1909), pp. 169–70.

5. The arguments in favor of divorce for the protection of women were advocated by such diverse individuals as feminists Ellen Key, Elizabeth Cady Stanton, and Charlotte Perkins Gilman; radical Emma Goldman; Commissioner of Labor in 1885 Carroll D. Wright; Harvard psychologist Hugo Munsterberg; *Arena* editor Benjamin O. Flower; and Chicago sociologist E. A. Ross, to name a few. Opposed were religious leaders such as Samuel Dike, James Cardinal Gibbon, Dr. Charles Henderson, and other critics including Harvard Professor of Christian Morals Francis Peabody, essayist Anna B. Rogers, journalist Harriet Anderson, and Theodore Roosevelt. See William L. O'Neill, *Divorce in the Progressive Era* (New Haven, 1967), especially chaps. 1, 2 and 4.

6. See, for example, James H. S. Bossard and Thelma Dillon, "The Spatial distribution of Divorced Women—A Philadelphia Study," *American Journal of Sociology* 40 (January 1935): 503–7; Ernest R. Mowrer, "Family Disorganization and Mobility," *American Sociological Society Publication No. 23,* 1928, pp. 134–52; Harvey J. Locke, "Mobility and Family Disorganization," *American Sociological Review* 5 (August 1940): 489–94; Christopher Tieze, Paul Lemkau and Marcia Cooper, "Personality Disorder and Spatial Mobility," *American Journal of Sociology* 48 (July 1942): 29–39; Elsa S. Longmoor and Erle F. Young, "Ecological Interrelationship of Juvenile Delinquency," *American Journal of Sociology* 41 (March 1936): 598–610; Ernest W. Burgess and Leonard S. Cottrell, Jr., *Predicting Success or Failure in Marriage* (New York, 1939), p, 253;

Peter H. Rossi, *Why Families Move* (Glencoe, Ill., 1955), pp. 1–10, 41, 71, 80–81, 155, 172. Recent studies have demonstrated that urban characteristics such as a high rate of geographical mobility were present long before the twentieth century—and long before the divorce rate began to rise dramatically. See for example Stephan Thernstrom, *The Other Bostonians* (Cambridge, Mass., 1973), chap. 9.

7. See Nelson M. Blake, *The Road to Reno* (New York, 1962); James H. Barnett, *Divorce and the American Divorce Novel,* (Philadelphia, 1939), esp. chap. 1, "Divorce Legislation and Trends."

8. Alfred A. Cahen, *A Statistical Analysis of American Divorce* (New York, 1932), pp. 88–89; Blake, *Road to Reno,* pp. 233–34.

9. Wendy McDowell Healy, "The Divorce Scare in New Jersey, 1890–1925: A Study in Causation and Legislation," senior thesis, Princeton University, 1976.

10. Cahen, *Statistical Analysis,* p. 92.

11. See for example Walter Willcox, *The Divorce Problem, A Study in Social Causation* (New York, 1891), p. 61.

12. Blake, *Road to Reno,* p. 81.

13. See George E. Mowry, *The California Progressives* (Berkeley, 1951).

14. William O'Neill, for example, considers divorce the "safety valve that makes the system workable . . . not an anomaly or a flaw in the system, but an essential feature of it." *Divorce,* pp. 6–7. Christopher Lasch has written, "It is quite possible that easier divorce, far from threatening the family, has actually helped to preserve it as a dominant institution of modern society." See Lasch, "Divorce and the Family in America," *Atlantic Monthly,* November 1966, pp. 57–61. Donald Meyer has perceived that divorce "has come to be seen generally not as a 'necessary evil' . . . but as a positive good. . . . " He further suggests that divorce is the natural result of a strict sexual ethic: "Churches clearly prefer immature marriages and a high divorce rate to mature marriages, a lower divorce rate, and sex for the unmarried young." See Meyer, "Churches and Families," in William McLaughlin and Robert N. Bellah, eds., *Religion in America* (Boston, 1968), pp. 230–48.

15. O'Neill, *Divorce,* pp. 24–25.

16. Although 1920 was a postwar year, few cases include conflicts resulting directly from the war. The upward trend in the divorce rate began before the war, and continued until after the Depression. See table 1.

17. United States Department of Commerce, Bureau of the Census, *Population* 3 (Washington, D.C., 1920), p. 82.

18. James Q. Wilson, "Los Angeles Is—And Is Not—Different," in Werner Z. Hirsch, ed., *Los Angeles: Viability and Prospects for Metropolitan Leadership* (New York, 1971), p. 123.

19. United States Department of Commerce, Bureau of the Census, *Marriage and Divorce, 1916* (Washington, D.C., 1919), pp. 39, 40.

CHAPTER ONE

1. Dana W. Bartlett, *The Better City: A Sociological Study of a Modern City* (Los Angeles, 1907), p. 11.

2. Recently, scholars such as Ann Douglas, Nancy Cott, Carl Degler, Daniel Scott Smith, and others have begun to reevaluate Victorianism vis-à-vis modern life and challenge some of the clichés surrounding nineteenth-century society. Christopher Lasch has noted that "we tend to exaggerate the moral distance between ourselves and the Victorians." Lasch, "Divorce and the Family," p. 57.

3. This is drawn from a large body of writings on the social and cultural developments of the eighteenth century. For a few suggestive readings, see Linda K. Kerber, "Daughters of Columbia: Educating Women for the Republic, 1787–1805," in Stanley Elkins and Eric McKitrick, eds., *The Hofstadter Aegis* (New York, 1974); James A. Henretta, "Economic Development and Social Structure in Colonial Boston," *William and Mary Quarterly*, 3d ser. 22 (1965): 75–92; Philip J. Greven, *Four Generations: Population, Land and Family in Colonial Andover, Massachusetts* (Ithaca, 1970); Richard L. Bushman, *From Puritan to Yankee* (New York, 1967); Page Smith, *Daughters of the Promised Land* (Boston, 1970); Richard D. Brown, *Modernization: The Transformation in American Life, 1600–1685* (New York, 1976), especially chap. 3.

4. Quotes are from Ebenezer Baily, *The Young Ladies Class Book* (Boston, 1831), p. 168; and William Alcott, *The Young Man's Guide* (Boston, 1833), pp. 299, 231. There is a rich literature on nineteenth-century sex roles. For a few examples, see Smith, *Daughters;* Nancy Cott, *The Bonds of Womanhood* (New Haven, 1977); Carroll Smith-Rosenberg, "The Female World of Love and Ritual: Relations Between Women in Nineteenth-Century America," Barbara Welter, "The Cult of True Womanhood: 1820–1860," G. J. Barker-Benfield, "The Spermatic Economy: A Nineteenth-Century View of Sexuality," all in Michael Gordon, ed., *The American Family in Social-Historical Perspective*, 2d ed. (New York, 1978). For primary sources, see any novels by Horatio Alger or James Fenimore Cooper, magazines such as *Godey's Lady's Book,* sermons and tracts by Russel Conwell or Josiah Strong, testimonies collected in Nancy Cott, ed., *Root of Bitterness* (New York, 1972), chap. 3. For an excellent description of Victorianism from the inside, especially the way in which male and female sex roles intertwined, see Henry Seidel Canby, *The Age of Confidence* (New York, 1934).

5. See for example Kathryn K. Sklar, *Catharine Beecher: A Study in American Domesticity*, (New York, 1976); Gerda Lerner, *The Grimke Sisters* (New York, 1971); Cott, *Bonds of Womanhood;* Andrew Sinclair, *The Emancipation of the American Woman* (New York, 1965); Estelle Freedman, *Their Sisters' Keepers: Women's Prison Reform in America, 1830–1930* (University of Michigan Press, Ann Arbor, forthcoming).

6. Alexis de Tocqueville, *Democracy in America* (New York, 1945 ed.), especially vol. 2.

7. See for example Whitney R. Cross, *The Burned Over District* (New York, 1950); Richard D. Brown *Modernization: The Transformation of American Life, 1600–1865* (New York, 1976), p. 108; Richard P. McCormick, *The Second American Party System: Party Formation in the Jacksonian Era* (Chapel Hill, N.C., 1966), pp. 350–351; Eric Foner, *Free Soil, Free Labor, Free Men,* (New York, 1970).

8. See Susan E. Hirsch, *Roots of the American Working Class: The Industrialization of Crafts in Newark, 1800–1860* (Philadelphia, 1978); and Paul E. Johnson, *A Shopkeeper's Millennium: Society and Revivals in Rochester, New York, 1815–1837 (New York, 1978).*

9. Herbert G. Gutman, *Work, Culture, and Society in Industrializing America* (New York, 1976).

10. See for example Stephan Thernstrom, *Poverty and Progress* (Cambridge, Mass., 1964). The tensions between reformers and ethnics are illustrated in William L. Riordan, *Plunkitt of Tammany Hall* (New York, 1963 ed.); and Margaret Byington, *Homestead: The Households of a Mill Town* (Pittsburgh, 1910).

11. See Canby, *Age of Confidence*.

12. See for example Henry Nash Smith, *The Virgin Land,* New York, 1950); Frederick Jackson Turner, *The Frontier in American History* (New York, 1920).

CHAPTER TWO

1. United States Bureau of the Census, *Population* 3 (Washington, D.C., 1920): 82.

2. Robert M. Fogelson, *The Fragmented Metropolis: Los Angeles 1850–1930* (Cambridge, Mass., 1967) pp. 121, 123. Sam Bass Warner notes that Los Angeles did not become committed to manufacturing until the 1940s and lacked a fully elaborated industrial region until then. See Sam Bass Warner, Jr., *The Urban Wilderness* (New York, 1972), p. 135.

3. Carey McWilliams, *Southern California Country, an Island on the Land* (New York, 1946), p. 129.

4. George E. Mowry, *The California Progressives* (Berkeley, 1951), pp. 6–7; Gregory H. Singleton, *Religion in the City of Angeles: American Protestant Culture and Urbanization, Los Angeles, 1850–1930* (Ann Arbor, 1979).

5. Resolution of Illinois Association of Los Angeles, December 1886, in McWilliams, *Southern California Country,* p. 166.

6. McWilliams, *Southern California Country,* p. 96.

7. Singleton, *Religion,* pp. 145, 191–92; Gilman M. Ostrander, *The Prohibition Movement in California, 1848–1933* (Berkeley, 1957), pp. 77, 131.

8. Bartlett, *The Better City* p. 16.

9. Case 4191, Los Angeles, 1885.

10. Case 2773, Los Angeles, 1883.

11. Caroline Dall, *Woman's Right to Labour: Or Low Wages and Hard Work* (Boston, 1860), p. 104.

12. Case 4132, Los Angeles, 1882.

13. Case 2138, Los Angeles, 1883.

14. Alexis de Tocqueville, *Democracy in America,* (New York, 1945 ed.) 2: 212, 249.

15. Lary L. May, *Screening Out the Past: The Birth of Mass Culture and the Motion Picture Industry* (Oxford University Press, New York, 1980).

16. Case 1859, Los Angeles, 1882.

17. Case 4316, Los Angeles, 1885.

18. Case 2494, Los Angeles, 1883, resolution unclear.

19. Case 4431, Los Angeles, 1885.

20. Case 2348, Los Angeles, 1883.

21. For example, cases 3378 and 2916, both Los Angeles, 1884, and case 5348, Los Angeles, 1886.

22. Case 5348, Los Angeles, 1886.

23. Case 4417, Los Angeles, 1885.

24. Case 393, Los Angeles, 1880.

25. Case 3245, Los Angeles, 1884.

26. Case 3672, Los Angeles, 1884.

27. Case 5147, Los Angeles, 1886.

28. Case 5328, Los Angeles, 1886.

29. Case 3759, Los Angeles, 1885.

30. Case 3904, Los Angeles, 1885.

31. Case 2949, Los Angeles, 1884.

32. Tocqueville, *Democracy,* 2:212.

33. Case 5429, Los Angeles, 1883.

34. Case 3540, Los Angeles, 1884.

35. Case 3899, Los Angeles, 1885.

36. Case 5097, Los Angeles, 1886.

37. Case 1066, Los Angeles, 1881.

38. Case 1652, Los Angeles, 1882.

39. Case 2656, Los Angeles, 1883.

40. Case 5103, Los Angeles, 1886.

41. Case 5120, Los Angeles, 1885.

42. Case 4397, Los Angeles, 1886.

43. Case 2578, Los Angeles, 1883.

44. Case 2419, Los Angeles, 1882.

45. Case 5205, Los Angeles, 1886.

46. Case 3449, Los Angeles, 1884.

47. Case 4165, Los Angeles, 1885.

48. Case 4562, Los Angeles, 1885.

49. Cases 2478, Los Angeles, 1883; 1305, Los Angeles, 1880.

50. Case 4718, Los Angeles, 1886.

51. Case 2897, Los Angeles, 1884.

52. Canby, *Age of Confidence,* pp. 27–29.

CHAPTER THREE

1. Richard Hofstadter, *The Age of Reform* (New York, 1955), pp. 217–218.

2. See for example C. Wright Mills, *White Collar* (New York, 1956);

Robert S. Lynd and Helen Merrell Lynd, *Middletown* (New York, 1956), chaps. 4–8; Edward Kirkland, *Dream and Thought in the Business Community, 1860–1900* (New York, 1956); Daniel Miller and Guy Swanson, *The Changing American Parent* (New York, 1958), links the increased security to changes in family life. For a discussion of the scholarly debate, see Donald Meyer, "Churches and Families," in William McLaughlin, ed., *Religion in America* (Boston, 1968).

3. Bureau of the Census, *Population* 2 (Washington, D.C., 1920): 22, 33; William Henry Chafe, *The American Woman* (New York, 1972), p. 56.

4. Department of Commerce, *Historical Statistics of the United States* (Washington, D.C., 1960), pp. 139, 179; Thorstein Veblen, *The Theory of the Leisure Class* (New York, 1967 ed.), pp. 87, 111.

5. *National Municipal Review* 4 (July 1915): 419.

6. *National Municipal Review* 4 (October 1915): 124; ibid., 4 (July 1916): 485.

7. J. G. Woods, "The Progressives and the Police," Ph.D. diss., University of California at Los Angeles, 1973, p. 88.

8. George H. Dunlop, "Proportional Representation at Los Angeles," *National Municipal Review* 3 (January 1914): 92–95.

9. Mowry, *The California Progressives*, pp. 96–97.

10. Bartlett, *The Better City*, p. 83.

11. Ibid., pp. 71, 74.

12. See Sam Bass Warner, Jr., *Streetcar Suburbs* Cambridge, Mass. 1962).

13. William L. Bailey, "The Twentieth Century City," *American City*, August 1924, pp. 142–43.

14. Waldon Fawcett, "Suburban Life in America," *Cosmopolitan*, July 1903, pp. 309–16, emphasis added.

15. For discussions of the nature of suburbia, see for example Thomas Ktsaɾᵉˢ and Leonard Reissman, "Suburbia—New Homes for Old Values," ˳˳ ial Problems 7 (Winter 1959–60): 187–94; Scott Grier, "Social Structure and Political Process of Suburbia," *American Sociological Review* 25 (August 1960): 514–26; Leo F. Schnore, "Metropolitan Growth and Decentralization," *American Journal of Sociology* 63 (September 1957): 171–79, and "The Growth of Metropolitan Suburbs," *American Sociological Review* 23, (April 1957): 165–73; Warner, *Streetcar Suburbs;* William M. Dobriner, ed., *The Suburban Community,* (New York, 1958).

16. Warner, *The Urban Wilderness*, p. 29; Fawcett, "Suburban Life," p. 314.

17. Mc Williams, *Southern California Country*, p. 96.

18. Bartlett, *Better City*, p. 84.

CHAPTER FOUR

1. Cecil B DeMille, *Why Change Your Wife* (1919).

2. Robert S. Lynd and Helen M. Lynd, *Middletown* (New York, 1956), pp. 117, 241.

3. U.S. Bureau of the Census, *Historical Statistics of the United*

States (Washington, D.C., 1960), p. 15; and Paul H. Jacobson, *American Marriage and Divorce* (New York, 1959), p. 21.

4. Jacobson, *Marriage and Divorce,* p. 71.

5. *The Age Factor in Selling and Advertising, A Study in a New Phase of Advertising* (New York: Photoplay, 1922), pp. 1–27.

6. Lavinia Hart, "What Love Is," *Cosmopolitan,* July 1903, p. 261.

7. Lynd and Lynd, *Middletown,* p. 117.

8. Gene Sheridan, "The Lost Romance," *Photoplay,* July 1921, p. 39.

9. Preston W. Slosson, *The Great Crusade and After,* (New York, 1931), p. 155.

10. Advertisement, *Photoplay,* July 1921, p. 10.

11. Penrhyn Stanlaus, "The Art of Dress," *Photoplay,* April 1921, p. 49.

12. Lynd and Lynd, *Middletown,* p. 117.

13. E. Lloyd Sheldon, "The New Profession of Beauty," *Delineator,* March 1916, p. 5.

14. Kenneth A. Yellis, "Prosperity's Child: Some Thoughts on the Flapper," *American Quarterly* 21 (Spring 1969): 49.

15. Elinor Glyn, "In Filmdom's Boudoir," *Photoplay,* March 1921, p. 29.

16. Ibid.

17. Elizabeth Bisland, "The Modern Woman and Marriage," *North American Review,* June 1895, p. 754.

18. Edward Bok, "What Should a Young Wife Stand For?" *Ladies Home Journal,* July 1902, p. 18; Advertisement, *Ladies Home Journal,* December 1901, back cover.

19. Lavinia Hart, "The Way to Win a Woman," *Cosmopolitan,* August 1903, p. 399.

20. Antonio Moreno, "Confessions of a Modern Don Juan," *Photoplay,* May 1921, p. 46.

21. Lynd and Lynd, *Middletown,* p. 111.

22. Matthew J. Brucoli and Jackson R. Bryer, eds., *F. Scott Fitzgerald, In His Own Time: A Miscellany* (New York, 1971), p. 207; for a discussion of this theme, see Lewis A. Erenberg, *Steppin' Out: New York Night Life and the Decline of Victorianism, 1890–1930* (Greenwood Press, forthcoming).

23. Mark Sullivan, *Our Times,* 4 vols. (New York, 1932) 4:234.

24. Quoted in Bob Duncan and Wanda Duncan, *Castles in the Air* (New York, 1958), p. 87.

25. See May, *Screening Out the Past.*

26. Lynd and Lynd, *Middletown,* p. 120, emphasis added.

27. Wallace Reid, "How To Hold a Wife," *Photoplay,* January 1921, pp. 28–30.

28. George A. Bartlett, *Men, Women and Conflict* (New York, 1931), pp. 55, 67.

29. Dorothy Phillips, "How To Hold Him," *Photoplay,* November 1920, p. 46.

30. Ruth A. Cavan, *The American Family* (New York, 1969), pp. 25–26.

31. Lavinia Hart, "When Woman's Ideals Fall," *Cosmopolitan,* December 1902, pp. 695–96.

CHAPTER FIVE

1 May, *Screening Out the Past.*
2. Adela Rogers St. Johns, "The Married Life of Doug and Mary," *Photoplay,* February 1927, pp. 34, 134–36.
3. Case H–60–199, New Jersey, 1920.
4. Case D452, Los Angeles, 1920.
5. Case D484, Los Angeles, 1920.
6. Case D490, Los Angeles, 1920.
7. Case D345, Los Angeles, 1920.
8. Case D190, Los Angeles, 1920.
9. Case D136, Los Angeles, 1920.
10. Case D332, Los Angeles, 1920.
11. Case D476, Los Angeles, 1920.
12. Case D486, Los Angeles, 1920.
13. Case D239, Los Angeles, 1920.
14. Interview with the author's grandmother-in-law Mrs. June Glassmeyer, 12 July 1974.
15. Case D104, Los Angeles, 1920.
16. Case D216, Los Angeles, 1920, proceedings incomplete.
17. Bartlett, *Men, Women and Conflict,* pp. 55, 67.
18. Case G–60–0134, New Jersey, 1920.
19. Case H–60–1206, New Jersey, 1920.
20. Cases X–48–152, C–60–309, C–60–307, X–53–132, G–60–703, all New Jersey, 1920.
21. Case F–60–464, New Jersey, 1920.
22. Case Z–60–214, New Jersey, 1920.
23. Case X–59–546, New Jersey, 1920.
24. James G. Powers, *Marriage and Divorce* (New York, 1870), p. 97.
25. Case D436, Los Angeles, 1920.
26. Case D346, Los Angeles, 1920.
27. See, for example, John and Virginia Demos, "Adolescence in Historical Perspective," in Gordon, *The American Family,* pp. 209–22.
28. Case D199, Los Angeles, 1920. This case also included conflicts and disagreements over the raising of children, such as the husband's anger that their daughter married "beneath her station in life."

CHAPTER SIX

1. Quote is from an advertisement for *Sexual Lovemaking,* in Page Smith, *Daughters of the Promised Land,* (Boston, 1970), p. 241. The ideal of premarital chastity persists today. In an interesting case, the principal of Urbana High School in Ohio recently ruled that "only virgins can run for homecoming queen." See "Queen Ballot: 'Virgins Only,'" *Los Angeles Times,* 29 September 1973, p. 16.
2. Dio Lewis, *Chastity, or Our Secret Sins* (New York, 1871); Carl

Bode, "Columbia's Carnal Bed," *American Quarterly* 15 (Spring, 1963); Henry James, "Is Marriage Holy?" *Nation* (26 May, 1890), pp. 332–33.

3. T. S. Arthur, *Advice to Young Men on their Duties and Conduct in Life* (Boston, 1849), p. 178.

4. Alexis de Tocqueville, in Richard D. Heffner, ed., *Democracy in America* (New York, 1956), p. 235.

5. Daniel Scott Smith, "Premarital Pregnancy in America, 1640–1971: An Overview and Interpretation," *Journal of Interdisciplinary History* (Winter, 1975).

6. Barker-Benfield, "The Spermatic Economy," pp. 336–72.

7. Daniel Scott Smith, "The Dating of the American Sexual Revolution," in Gordon, *American Family,* p. 322.

8. Lewis M. Terman et al., "Psychological Factors in Marital Happiness" (New York, 1938), in W. F. Ogburn, *Technology and the Changing Family* (New York, 1955), p. 51; Alfred C. Kinsey, Wardwell B. Pomeroy, and Clyde E. Martin, *Sexual Behavior in the Human Male* (Philadelphia, 1948), pp. 411–13.

9. D. S. Smith, "The Dating of the American Sexual Revolution," pp. 331–32.

10. Ogburn, *Technology,* p. 51.

11. Lynd and Lynd, *Middletown,* p. 112.

12. Eleanore B. Luckey and Gilbert D. Nass, "Comparison of Sexual Attitudes in an International Sample of College Students," *Human Sexuality,* January 1972, pp. 85, 97, 102.

13. Case D321, Los Angeles, 1920.

14. Case D277, Los Angeles, 1920.

15. Fraud was usually charged in cases where one spouse had a valid previous marriage still in effect.

16. Case G–60–292, New Jersey, 1920.

17. Case G–60–400, New Jersey, 1920.

18. Case X–48–188, New Jersey, 1920.

19. Case G–60–335, New Jersey, 1920.

20. Case X–48–171, New Jersey, 1920.

21. Case X–48–206, New Jersey, 1920.

22. Case C–60–300, New Jersey, 1920.

23. Case G–60–674, New Jersey, 1920. Similar comments are found in cases G–60–267, and X–59–619, both New Jersey, 1920.

24. Tennie C. Clafin, *Constitutional Equality: A Right of Women,* (New York, 1871), p. 75.

25. Victoria Woodhull, *The Human Body, The Temple of God* (London, 1890), pp. 29–31, 51, 53.

26. Smith, *Daughters,* p. 239.

27. There were a few outspoken individuals, such as Emma Goldman, who went beyond this and fiercely criticized the society's sexual mores. But they never gained even a modicum of respectability outside radical circles.

28. Margaret Sanger, *Autobiography* (New York, 1938), pp. 1–2.

29. Sanger *Pivot of Civilization* (New York, 1922), pp. 140, 258.

Havelock Ellis shared these views. See Arthur Calder-Marshall, *The Sage of Sex: A Life of Havelock Ellis* (New York, 1959); David M. Kennedy, *Birth Control in America* (New Haven, 1970), pp. 29, 99.

30. Benjamin O. Flower, "Prostitution Within the Marriage Bond," *Arena* 13 (1895): 66–67.

31. Case D266, Los Angeles, 1920.

32. Case D218, Los Angeles, 1920.

33. Case D495, Los Angeles, 1920.

34. Case X–59–623, New Jersey, 1920.

35. Case G–60–334, New Jersey, 1920.

36. Case D41, Los Angeles, 1920.

37. Case D40, Los Angeles, 1920. New Jersey cases involved similar conflicts. See for example case C–60–34, New Jersey, 1920.

38. Case D290, Los Angeles, 1920.

39. Case B–48–631, New Jersey, 1920.

40. For a discussion of the early development of these attitudes, see Winthrop D. Jordan, *White Over Black* (Baltimore, 1968), especially chap. 4, "Fruits of Passion."

41. Case D54, Los Angeles, 1920.

42. A recent study of openness concerning intimate marital problems suggests that this may have been the case. See John E. Mayer, *The Disclosure of Marital Problems—An Exploratory Study of Lower and Middle-Class Wives* (New York, 1966).

43. Case D253, Los Angeles, 1920.

44. Case D342, Los Angeles, 1920.

45. Case D28, Los Angeles, 1920.

46. Case D244, Los Angeles, 1920.

47. Case F–60–473, New Jersey, 1920.

48. Kennedy, *Birth Control,* p. 170.

CHAPTER SEVEN

1. Charlotte Perkins Gilman, *The Home, Its Work and Influence* (New York, 1910), pp. 270–71.

2. Canby, *The Age of Confidence,* p.34.

3. Edward Bok, *Ladies Home Journal,* March, 1900, p. 16.

4. Frederic C. Howe, *The Confessions of a Reformer* (New York, 1925), pp. 66–69, 233–35.

5. Edward Chase Kirkland, *Industry Comes of Age* (New York, 1961), p. 331; Chafe, *The American Woman,* p. 100.

6. Chafe, *American Woman,* p. 56.

7. Lynd and Lynd, *Middletown,* pp. 80–81.

8. Healy, "The Divorce Scare," p. 62.

9. Case D322, Los Angeles, 1920.

10. Case D346, Los Angeles, 1920.

11. Case X–48–177, New Jersey, 1920.

12. Case F–60–467, New Jersey, 1920.

13. Cases H–60–208; H–60–235; G–60–680; G–60–352, all New Jersey, 1920.

14. Case C–60–302, New Jersey, 1920.

15. Case D446, Los Angeles, 1920.
16. Case D87, Los Angeles, 1920.
17. Case D382, Los Angeles, 1920.
18. Case H–60–433, New Jersey, 1920.
19. Case Z–60–226, New Jersey, 1920.
20. Case X–59–628, New Jersey, 1920.
21. Case G–60–226, New Jersey, 1920.
22. Case D412, Los Angeles, 1920.
23. Case D29, Los Angeles, 1920.
24. Case D138, Los Angeles, 1920.
25. Gilman, *The Home*, p. 292.
26. Bartlett, *Men, Women and Conflict*, p. 222.

CHAPTER EIGHT

1. Lynd and Lynd, *Middletown*, 1956, pp. 80–81, 126. Nationally, the percentage of divorces granted for "neglect to provide" rose steadily from 1870 to 1930, and then declined up to 1950. Jacobson, *Marriage and Divorce*, p. 126.

2. Bartlett, *Men, Women, and Conflict*, pp. 201, 203, 306.

3. Edward Chase Kirkland, *Industry Comes of Age* (New York, 1961), p. 268; see also Mills, *White Collar*, chap. 8, pp. 263–64, 403.

4. Frank Presbrey, *The History and Development of Advertising* (Garden City, 1921), p. 341.

5. Bartlett, *Men, Women, and Conflict*, p. 79.

6. Ibid., p. 29.

7. Agnes Smith, "Do They Marry for Money?" *Photoplay*, December 1926, p. 38.

8. Case D251, Los Angeles, 1920.

9. Case D127, Los Angeles, 1920, emphasis added.

10. For discussions of social mobility in America, see Thernstrom, *Poverty and Progress*, and idem, *The Other Bostonians* (Cambridge, Mass., 1973); William Miller, ed., *Men in Business, Essays on the Historical Role of the Entrepreneur* (New York, 1962), esp. articles by Miller, Frances Gregory, and Irene Neu; Reinhard Bendix and Seymour M. Lipset, eds., *Social Mobility in Industrial Society* (Berkeley, 1959), esp. article by Bendix and Frank Howton. An intriguing exception is reported by Herbert G. Gutman in "The Reality of the Rags to Riches 'Myth': The Case of the Paterson, New Jersey, Locomotive, Iron, and Machinery Manufacturers, 1830–80," in Stephan Thernstrom and Richard Sennett, eds., *Nineteenth Century Cities* (New Haven, 1969). For an excellent discussion of economic independence as a central core of nineteenth-century republican ideology, see Eric Foner, *Free Soil*, especially chap. 1.

11. For a discussion of this trend, see Arno Mayer, "The Lower Middle Class As Historical Problem," *Journal of Modern History* 47, no. 3 (September 1975): 409–36.

12. Table 19 gives the total number of cases from which these patterns were drawn. Although few in number, these cases show striking variations.

13. Case D385, Los Angeles, 1920.
14. Case D177, Los Angeles, 1920.
15. Case D386, Los Angeles, 1920.
16. Kirkland *Industry,* p. 403.
17. Testimony of Samuel Gompers, *Report of the Industrial Commission* 8: 645, in Kirkland, *Industry,* p. 402.
18. Case D258, Los Angeles, 1920, emphasis added.
19. Case G–60–402, New Jersey, 1920.
20. Case H–60–193, New Jersey, 1920.
21. Case G–60–75, New Jersey, 1920.
22. Case H–60–186, New Jersey, 1920.
23. Case Z–60–202, New Jersey, 1920.
24. Case H–60–215, New Jersey, 1920.
25. Jacobson, *Marriage and Divorce,* pp. 126–27.
26. Ibid., p. 127.
27. Seventeen out of the 107 husbands required to pay alimony in the 1920 Los Angeles sample either complained about the amount or resisted making payments.
28. Case D269, Los Angeles, 1920.
29. Case D375, Los Angeles, 1920. This same principle was applied more recently, in the 1970s, in the divorce of Elvis and Priscilla Presley. See *Santa Monica Evening Outlook,* 30 May 1973, p. 26.

EPILOGUE
1. Bartlett, *Men, Women, and Conflict,* pp. v, 5.
2. Case D492, Los Angeles, 1920. Marsha Linganfield claimed that she refused sex in order to prevent pregnancy. But a number of other means of contraception were widely used at the time; her desire for "no brats" may well have been a convenient excuse.
3. Case D93, Los Angeles, 1920.
4. Case D91, Los Angeles, 1920.
5. Case D245, Los Angeles, 1920.
6. Case D310, Los Angeles, 1920.
7. Case D230, Los Angeles, 1920.
8. Case D301, Los Angeles, 1920.
9. The actual divorce statistics do not even include all cases brought to court. In the 1920 Los Angeles sample, for example, 20 percent of all cases were dismissed and 10 percent denied. Only about two thirds of the couples who came to court ended up legally divorced.
10. In the 1920 sample from Los Angeles, the average length of time the couples stayed together was eight years to separation and nine years to divorce. By the 1960s, divorce usually occurred after only one or two years of marriage. See Hugh Carter and Paul Glick, *Marriage and Divorce: A Social and Economic Study* (Cambridge, Mass., 1970), p. 35.

Index

Abolitionism, 54
Abortion, 90
Actresses, motion-picture, 65
Adolescents: love cult of, 62–63; sexual activity of, 96, 100
Adultery, 5, 8, 104, 122–23, 177; marital disappointment as cause of, 160; wives' jobs as cause of, 131
Advertising: and consumer ethic, rise of, 51, 139; and the Hollywood ideal, 63–64, 66–67
Affluence: blue-collar desires for 146–50; and consumer ethic, 137–40; growth of, 51–52, 57; in Hollywood ideal, 75–76; white-collar desires for, 140–46; and youth cult, 62–65, 68, 71
Aging. *See* the Hollywood ideal
Alger, Horatio, 17
Alimony, 150–55, 179–82
Amusements: in courtship ritual, 68–69, 71; Progressive reform of, 52–53; sexual segregation of, 29–33, 46, 81–82; wives attracted to, 41, 81–88, 94, 96–97; and work ethic, 20
Annulment, 8, 98; grounds for 177
Antivice laws, 26, 52–53, 58
Arena magazine, 103
Asceticism: decline of, 54, 58–59, 89, 113; economic basis of, 17–18, 28–29; sexual, 33, 36. *See also* Sexual gratification

Bartlett, Dana, on perfect family life, 55
Bartlett, George A., on brides, 70;

on divorce, 156; on modern affluence, 138, 139
Beauty cult. *See* the Hollywood ideal
Better City, The (Bartlett), 55
Birth control, 89, 101–2, 103
Blacks, 10, 109, 170
Blue-collar workers: and alimony, 151–52, 181–82; and consumer ethic, 50, 146–50; and divorce, 121–23, 134, 173, 177–79; sexual attitudes of, 110–11, 177; women as, 28, 51, 117, 118, 119–20
Bok, Edward, on working women, 116
Brutality, conjugal, 33–36, 38, 102–9, 176, 177
Bureaucracy, rise of, 50, 58, 142–44

Cabaret, 68–69, 82
California divorce laws, 5–6, 30, 104. *See also* Los Angeles
Castle, Irene and Vernon, 69
Catholics, 10, 21
Charity work, 18, 19–20
Chastity, 41–46, 87, 93–100, 156. *See also* Sex, premarital
Chicago, 9
Childrearing in modern family, 89
Children: and alimony awards, 124–25, 151, 152, 180; complaints involving, 176; custody of, 89, 175; as focus of family life. 88–90; Church attendance by Victorians, 18, 19, 20, 21, 24
Cities and urban living: as cause of divorce, 3, 25, 54; Los Angeles as

195